Against the Age

In memory of Howard Faulkner
1894–1979
artist and teacher

Against the Age

An Introduction to William Morris

PETER FAULKNER
School of English, University of Exeter

London
GEORGE ALLEN & UNWIN
Boston   Sydney

First published in 1980

GEORGE ALLEN & UNWIN LTD
40 Museum Street, London WC1A 1LU

© George Allen & Unwin (Publishers) Ltd, 1980

British Library Cataloguing in Publication Data

Faulkner, Peter
  Against the age.
  1. Morris, William, b. 1843 – Biography
  2. Authors, English – 19th century – Biography
  3. Artists – England – Biography
  I. Title
  709'.2'4   PR5083   80-40460

ISBN 0-04-809012-3

Set in 11 on 12 point Baskerville by Watford Typesetters
and printed and bound in Great Britain by
William Clowes (Beccles) Limited, Beccles and London

Contents

List of Illustrations

Between pages 84 and 85

Stained glass window photographed by Sonia Halliday
All other photographs Victoria and Albert Museum, Crown Copyright

Grateful acknowledgement is made

Preface

William Morris died in 1896 at the age of 62. By then he was widely known for many kinds of activity, for, much as he disliked the Renaissance, he had the many-sidedness of the ideal Renaissance man. He first made a reputation as a poet with *The Earthly Paradise* (1868–70); then 'the Firm', of which he was a founder and the main participant, became widely known for the quality of its work and the excellence of its design in stained glass, furnishings, wallpapers, textiles, tapestries and carpets; then he became a socialist, lecturing in many parts of the country on the relation of art and society, and arguing that Victorian capitalism was humanly and aesthetically disastrous; later he wrotes a series of strange, romantic stories in prose, and founded the Kelmscott Press, which gave a great impetus to the improvement of the art of printing. Thus his contribution to his age was on a grand scale – it is difficult to suggest a parallel figure in the twentieth century.

But Morris was not simply a great Victorian: he was a man who looked with care at the products and workings of society and who gave his energies to trying to improve them. The vision which he offered in *News from Nowhere,* the Utopian romance which brings together many of his most important concerns into an attractive story, is still worth our attention today. As long as our industrial society continues to perplex us with such problems as pollution, delinquency, commercial acquisitiveness and violence, so long will we stand in need of Morris's vision of a society of equals in which every man and woman finds proper fulfilment. The poet W. B. Yeats, who knew and admired Morris, wrote in 'The Happiest of the Poets' about the value of that vision:

> His vision is true because it is poetical, because we are a little happier when we are looking at it; and he knew as Shelley knew by an act of faith that the economists should take their measurements not from life as it is, but from the vision of men like that, from the vision

of the world made perfect that is buried under all minds.[1]

No society can possess a sense of direction unless it shares a vision of this kind, and it was Morris's distinction to try to create such a vision in the socialist movement of his day.

For Morris was above all a constructive worker, a man who never fulfilled the passive role which he gave himself in the Apology to *The Earthly Paradise* where he speaks of 'the idle singer of an empty day', and asks 'Why should I strive to set the crooked straight?' Biographers can try to answer this question, but the fact that Morris did so strive with all his formidable energies is obvious from the mere facts of his life. The writer Edward Carpenter wrote an obituary of Morris in the anarchist journal *Freedom* which defined very clearly Morris's outlook :

> He hated with a good loyal hatred all insincerity; but most he hated, and with his very soul, the ugliness and meanness of modern life. I believe that was the great inspiring hatred of his life.[2]

To be able to turn his hatred of commercial society into an inspiration was Morris's achievement, and marks him off from the aesthetes of the time who turned away from a society they found too unpleasant to contemplate. Morris was too involved with humanity, too passionate in his belief that a man's daily work should be a source of satisfaction to him, to retreat into an ivory tower. He wanted to share the satisfactions which the life of creative activity gave him, and this is what makes him relevant to us when we contemplate our own wasting world.

Anyone writing on Morris now is indebted to a large number of predecessors, above all to May Morris, the editor of the twenty-four fine volumes of the *Collected Works,* and to J. W. Mackail, Morris's first biographer; their books and others from which I have profited will be found in the Notes and Suggested Reading at the end of this book. Since my intention has been primarily to interest new readers in Morris, the emphasis is, however, mainly on his own work rather than on modern scholars' (or my own) views of it. In order to give some idea of the range of his achievement, I have quoted freely from his writings, especially as only a limited range of these is currently in print; while the illustrations should serve as a reminder of his non-literary activities. I have also tried to give some idea of how Morris struck his contemporaries, by quoting their views of him as he developed. My hope is that this introduction will lead readers to want to develop their knowledge of a great Victorian who has much of value to say to us today.

I

Early Life and Poetry, 1835–59

In 1883 Morris wrote a long letter to an Austrian refugee and socialist, Andreas Scheu, in which he gave a lively account of his life that cannot be improved upon as far as it goes. Quotations from the letter have been used to begin each chapter of this book.[1] The section covering his early years is characteristically clear and informal:

> I was born at Walthamstow in Essex in March 1834, a suburban village on the edge of Epping Forest, and once a pleasant place enough, but now terribly cocknified and choked up by the jerry-builder.
>
> My father was a business man in the city, and well-to-do; and we lived in the ordinary bourgeois style of comfort; and since we belonged to the evangelical section of the English Church I was brought up in what I should call rich establishmentarian puritanism; a religion which even as a boy I never took to.
>
> I went to school at Marlborough College, which was then a new and very rough school. As far as my school instruction went, I think I may fairly say I learned next to nothing there, for indeed next to nothing was taught; but the place is in very beautiful country,

1

thickly scattered over with prehistoric monuments, and I set myself eagerly to studying these and everything else that had any history in it, and so perhaps learned a good deal, especially as there was a good library at the school to which I sometimes had access. I should mention that ever since I could remember I was a great devourer of books. I don't remember being taught to read, and by the time I was seven years old I had read a very great many books, good, bad, and indifferent.

My father died in 1847 a few months before I went to Marlborough; but as he had engaged in a fortunate mining speculation before his death, we were left very well off, rich in fact.

I went to Oxford in 1853 as a member of Exeter College; I took very ill to the studies of the place, but fell-to very vigorously on history and especially mediaeval history, all the more perhaps because at this time I fell under the influence of the High Church or Puseyite school; that latter phase however did not last me long, as it was corrected by the books of John Ruskin which were at the time a sort of revelation to me; I was also a good deal influenced by the works of Charles Kingsley, and got into my head therefrom some socio-political ideas which would have developed probably but for the attractions of art and poetry. While I was still an undergraduate, I discovered that I could write poetry, much to my own amazement; and about that time being very intimate with other young men of enthusiastic ideas, we got up a monthly paper which lasted (to my cost) for a year; it was called the *Oxford and Cambridge Magazine,* and was very *young* indeed. When I had gone through my schools at Oxford, I who had been originally intended for the Church made up my mind to take to art in some form, and so articled myself to G. E. Street (the architect of the new Law Courts afterwards) who was then practising in Oxford; I only stayed with him nine months however, when being in London and having been introduced by Burne-Jones, the painter, who was my great college friend, to Dante Gabriel Rossetti, the leader of the Pre-Raphaelite School, I made up my mind to turn painter, and studied the art but in a very desultory way for some time.

Meantime in 1858 I published a volume of poems *The Defence of Guenevere;* exceedingly young also and very mediaeval.

Although Morris writes with some amusement over the naïveté of his youth, this account is accurate. Above all, it gives an impression of his devotion to history, particularly the history of England. This became the central enthusiasm of his life, the source of his poetic inspiration and the basis for his utopian vision.

The comfortable circumstances of his early life were due to his father's success in business, in particular to a fortunate investment in Great Devon Consuls, which rose at one time to a value of some £200,000. This enabled Mr Morris to acquire Woodford Hall, a substantial Georgian house, with spacious grounds, in 1840, and the family to move to Water House, Walthamstow (now the William Morris Gallery) in 1848, the year after Mr Morris's death. Living on the borders of Epping Forest, the young Morris was able to wander freely, at one time in a miniature suit of armour, often inventing stories of chivalry and adventure partly based on the reading of romantic novels – he had read most of those of Scott by the age of 7. The hornbeams of Epping were to feature in many of his descriptions of landscapes, while the vision of the past encouraged by Scott was to contribute substantially to his criticisms of Victorian England. Morris was a thick-set and energetic child and youth, excitable, restless, awkward and sensitive. Although he had four brothers and four sisters, he does not seem to have been very close to any of them except Emma, to whom some of his earliest letters were written. Her marriage in 1852 seems to have left him with a strong feeling of isolation. Although Morris throughout his life gave observers the impression of self-sufficiency because of his involvement in so many different types of work, this may have been misleading. His emotions were not the less deep because they were often concealed.

At Marlborough from 1845 to 1851 the poor organisation of the school, which actually led to a revolt of the pupils, allowed him to live in his own way, cultivating his enthusiasm for the English past and inventing imaginative stories. His physical energy led him into vigorous walking, and to such exercises as single-sticks, at which he was a dangerous antagonist. His creative energy had a clear physical basis; he could never bear to be idle. The school library contained works of archaeology and ecclesiastical history, including *Contrasts* by A. W. N. Pugin, a leading Roman Catholic mediaevalist and architect. Pugin's argument was that modern England was in every way inferior to mediaeval England, and he enforced this view by means of polemical pairs of illustrations such as 'A Catholic town in 1440' and 'The same town in 1840'.[2]

The chapel at Marlborough also introduced Morris to the High Church forms of service which were replacing the staid Evangelicalism of his parents in many English churches at the time. This was the result of the movement which had begun at Oxford in the 1830s when John Henry Newman, John Keble and Edward Pusey led an attack on the lack of spiritual idealism in the Church of England. Newman regarded Keble's assize sermon of 14 July 1833 on 'National Apostasy' as the start of what was to be called the Oxford movement. In the same year Newman inaugurated the series of *Tracts for the Times* which gave the movement its alternative name of Tractarian and helped to stimulate discussion of many issues, such as the relation of church and state, which previous, more easy-going generations had ignored. The call for a new seriousness in the church, in consonance with its early traditions, called forth a wide and deeply felt response in the younger generation. The situation became more involved after Newman had been received into the Roman Catholic Church in 1843, for this seemed to prove the validity of the argument put forward by opponents of the movement that it would lead its members away from the Church of England altogether, However, Keble, Pusey, and many others remained faithful to that church, and their teachings and examples became widely influential. The theology of the High Church movement laid emphasis on the priesthood and the sacraments, and consequently led to more interest in the liturgy and the church services themselves. All this must have appealed to sensitive and idealistic young men like Morris, and he was further encouraged in the direction by the Reverend F. B. Guy, who coached him for Oxford after he had left Marlborough in 1852, and by his favourite sister Emma.

The England in which Morris grew up, and which was to impinge more and more directly on him throughout his life, was a country rapidly becoming industrialised. The enormous development of the railways in the 1840s was obvious evidence of this. In the process of becoming wealthy, England was also becoming dirty and polluted, and the benefits of industrialisation were very unevenly spread. Some made fortunes, many were near starvation. The indignant accounts of the conditions of the urban poor given by novelists like Dickens and Mrs Gaskell and by social commentators like Carlyle and Engels remind us of how severe a shock industrialism was rendering to English society – the first to be fully exposed to such large-scale developments. Rural poverty was an age-old phenomenon, but the hideous squalor of the new cities was an appalling novelty. Kingsley and Ruskin, to whom Morris refers in his letter to Scheu, were among the authors most concerned to bring home to their readers the stark facts about the social changes so rapidly taking place. Charles Kingsley was associated with F. D. Maurice and others in the movement known as Christian Socialism, which aimed to save England from exploitative commercialism by a recall to the ethics of Christianity. Kingsley wrote many articles and pamphlets for this cause, and several novels. *Alton Locke, Tailor and Poet* (1850) is the fictional autobiography of a working man, a victim of the economic system, and is written with generous indignation, though little power of characterisation, and the same is true of *Yeast, a Problem* (1851). Kingsley's bluff, unsubtle personality had something in common with that of Morris, but the writings of John Ruskin were to exert a far more profound and lasting effect because they were concerned with art as well as society. Morris went up to Exeter College, Oxford, in January 1853 (though he was accepted for October 1852), where he evidently read the first two volumes of Ruskin's *Modern Painters* and discussed them with his friends, who included Edward Jones, later as Burne-Jones to become the well-known painter, and R. W. Dixon, poet and future cleric, who recalled Morris's 'chanting' of passages from Ruskin concerning the Slave Ship and Turner's skies. But Morris and Burne-Jones were even more impressed by *The Stones of Venice* (1851–3). The second volume

5

contains a chapter entitled 'Of the nature of Gothic' which represents the vital centre of Ruskin's social thinking; Morris was later to reprint it at the Kelmscott Press. In it Ruskin argues that man is only free when he can exercise his creative gifts in his work, and that this freedom has been destroyed by industrialism :

> Men were not intended to work with the accuracy of tools, to be precise and perfect in all their actions. If you will have that precision out of them, and make their fingers measure degrees like cog-wheels, and their arms strike curves like compasses, you must unhumanize them . . . there might be more freedom in England, though her feudal lords' lightest words were worth men's lives, and though the blood of the vexed husbandman dropped into the furrows of his fields, than there is while the animation of her multitudes is set like fuel to feed the factory smoke, and the strength of them is given daily to be wasted into the fineness of a web, or racked into the exactness of a line.[3]

This is powerful writing directed towards a central social problem of the time and we cannot be surprised that Morris and Burne-Jones (who came from Birmingham and had a closer knowledge of the realities of industrialism than his wealthier friend) were impressed by it, though it was not until later that its influence became apparent in Morris's work.

Morris found no stimulus in his academic work at Oxford, but enjoyed the architecture of the city, still so markedly mediaeval in character, and the opportunity to read and to talk with his friends. Reminiscences of the period, such as those of Dixon recorded by Mackail in his *Life of William Morris,* emphasise the energy with which Morris threw himself into many activities. As to his reading, Morris's own account is preserved in some notes by Sydney Cockerell :

> Our clique was much influenced by Keats, who was a poet who represented semblances, as opposed to Shelley who had no eyes, and whose admiration [i.e. admiration of whom] was not critical but conventional. I

6

remember the issue of Tennyson's 'Maud' [July 1855], and its doubtful reception by the reviewers. I went up to College in 1852. Ruskin's 'Stones of Venice' (vols. 2 and 3) came out in the following year, and made a deep impression. I read Mrs Browning a great deal at Oxford. She was a great poetess – in some respects she had greater capacity than Browning, though she was a poor rhymer. I refer to the earlier works; 'Aurora Leigh' I consider dull. I pretended to like Wordsworth at that time, and was to some extent touched by the Kingsley movement which, like Puseyism, was a reaction against Puritanism. I never read Byron . . .[4]

The modern reader may find it difficult to see what Morris saw in Elizabeth Barrett Browning's often sentimental poetry, but she was popular at the time for her gentle humanity. She had also modernised from Chaucer 'Queen Annelida and the False Arcite' in 1841, which may have stimulated Morris's interest in the mediaeval poet. It seems that Morris also enjoyed at this period Carlyle's polemic against the materialism of the age in *Past and Present* (1843), the folktales recorded in works like Benjamin Thorpe's three volumes of *Northern Mythology* (1851), the fantastic and bizarre stories of Edgar Allan Poe, and also writings associated with the High Church point of view, like Charlotte Yonge's *The Heir of Redclyffe*. Published early in 1853, this novel was a great popular success. Its essence is the development of Sir Guy Morville from an ill-disciplined, occasionally violent though well-meaning young man into a true Christian who dies as a result of catching fever watching at the bedside of a man who had disliked him. The way in which the novel Christianised the kind of Byronic hero to be found also in the novels of the Brontës was recognised by many readers as an eloquent message for the times. It is significant in relation to Morris that Guy is enthusiastic about Sir Galahad and Malory's 'two fat volumes' of the *Morte D'Arthur,* dismissed by one of the other characters as 'a strange mixture of religion and romance'; an artist later wants Guy to sit for him as a model for Galahad.

On 1 May 1853 Burne-Jones had written to his friend Cormell Price:

Remember I have set my heart upon our founding a Brotherhood. Learn 'Sir Galahad' [Tennyson's poem] by heart. He is to be the patron of our order. I have enlisted *one* in the project up here, heart and soul. You shall have a copy of the canons some day.

Characteristically, Morris found Tennyson's Galahad, according to Dixon, 'rather a mild youth', but he was certainly keen to join in some constructive action such as Burne-Jones was to style, in a letter to Price later that year, 'this crusade and Holy Warfare against the age'.[5] But as the young friends developed, this seemed less likely to take the form they had originally imagined, that of ordination, but rather to become associated with art.

Apart from reading and talking to his friends, and seeing some recent Pre-Raphaelite pictures and the mediaeval manuscripts in the Bodleian Library, the most important experiences of these years for Morris occurred as a result of his summer vacation tours. In 1854 he visited Belgium and northern France, and was deeply impressed by the paintings of Memling and Van Eyck, whose precision and vivid detail he was always to admire, and even more by the great cathedrals of Amiens, Beauvais, Chartres and Rouen. When he reverted in his lecture 'The aims of art', in 1887, to his first sight of Rouen, then still largely a mediaeval city, he could say that, 'looking back on my past life, it was the greatest pleasure I have ever had : and now it is a pleasure which no one can ever have again : it is lost to the world for ever'.[6] The final comment suggests the social criticism which was to become central to Morris; but in 1854 it was the simple, irresistible impact of great Gothic architecture which he recorded. The next summer he visited Abbeville, Amiens, Chartres and Rouen with Burne-Jones. On the way back the two young men decided not to enter the church, but rather to devote their lives to art. Burne-Jones's account, as recorded in the *Memorials,* is simple and moving :

It was while walking on the quay at Havre at night that we resolved definitely that we would begin a life of art, and put off our decision no longer – he should be an architect and I a painter. It was a resolve only needing final conclusion; we were bent on that road

8

for the whole past year, and after that night's talk we
never hesitated more. That was the most memorable
night of my life.[7]

The decision was crucial and, for Morris at least, inevitable. His
sensibility was not at all religious; his energies were now directed
to an end which he saw as directly human – an art envisioned
through the attractions of the Gothic architecture he loved in
opposition to modern industrial-commercial England. Soon after
their return to England, Burne-Jones showed Morris a copy of
Southey's edition of the *Morte D'Arthur* of Malory, that treasure-
house of Arthurian legend. Burne-Jones had been able only to
read it in the bookshop, but the wealthier Morris immediately
bought it. Its stories were to become the source of much of
Burne-Jones's art and some of Morris's poetry. Malory's work
had a curious history, no edition of it appearing between 1634
and 1816. In that year, however, two editions appeared, to be
followed by Southey's in 1817, and others later in the century.
Tennyson took a life-long interest in Arthurian stories, from 'The
Lady of Shalott' (1832), 'Morte D'Arthur' (1842) and 'Sir
Galahad' (1842), through the first series of *Idylls of the King*
in 1859 to the completion of the work in 1882; Bulwer Lytton
published *King Arthur, an Epic Fable in Twelve Books* in 1848.
It would seem that the Victorians discovered in these stories a
picturesque version of the English past which linked up with
other aspects of mediaevalism to provide some reassurance in a
period of disconcertingly rapid change. Painters, too, found
Malory an inspiration. This was particularly true of the Pre-
Raphaelites, the group led by Dante Gabriel Rossetti, John
Everett Millais and William Holman Hunt, whose appearance
in 1848 offered a direct challenge to academic art in its insistence
on accuracy of observation and vividness of colour. Morris and
Burne-Jones were led to these painters by reading Ruskin's
defence of them in his Edinburgh lectures of 1854, and were
most impressed by Rossetti's water-colour of Dante drawing the
head of Beatrice, which they saw in Oxford.

In 1855 Morris came of age and inherited £900 a year. With
the backing of this money, Morris and a group of friends decided
to launch a literary and artistic magazine, modelled to some
extent on *The Germ,* which had been produced by Rossetti and

other Pre-Raphaelites in 1850, though it had lasted only for four issues. *The Oxford and Cambridge Magazine* – so called because of its young contributors from the two universities – lasted for the whole of the year 1856. It was an attempt to express through writing the ideals which its contributors held as alternatives to the religious views they were leaving behind. It contained contributions on social as well as cultural matters. Morris himself wrote on Amiens Cathedral, Browning's *Men and Women* and the German wood-engraver Alfred Rendel, but his main contributions were seven prose stories whose air of mystery makes the description 'romances' appropriate, and one story of modern life. The romances show Morris's Romantic legacy clearly enough, and his interest in folk literature.[8] One of the most powerful and grotesque stories, 'Lindenborg Pool', is directly derived from Benjamin Thorpe's *Northern Mythology*. The narrator is a modern man who suddenly finds himself – a typical dream effect – in a strange world and a dreary setting. He is riding a mule and dressed as a priest, and he realises that he is now in the thirteenth century. He is induced to visit a lord, who is said to be dying, in his castle, but is aware of a strong and disturbing atmosphere. When he offers the sacred wafer for the sacrament, the 'lord' is revealed as 'a huge *swine*' which falls to the floor, enmeshed in the bedding, amid the coarse laughter of those present. The narrator makes his escape, 'yet could not, as in a dream, go fast enough'. The relief he feels on escaping from the mocking atmosphere is vividly conveyed in clear and simple language, and the story ends with the disappearance of the castle and its transformation into 'a deep black lake' – the Pool itself.

The story is one of the most successful because of its brevity and definite outline. In others like 'Gertha's Lovers' and 'The Hollow Land' the lack of narrative movement weakens the effect. But in all of the stories, which take place in either Nordic or mediaeval settings, the predominant feelings are of crisis. They are mostly concerned with love, but the lovers find themselves in worlds of ignorance, brutality and evil. It would be misleading to suggest that the sense of crisis in these romances was a direct expression of social concern. It no doubt owes much to Morris's own problems in growing into adulthood, deprived of the close friendship of his sister Emma by her unexpected marriage in 1852. But neither are they the work of a trivial man, or one who would ignore unpleasant realities wherever he might locate them. It is characteristic of Morris that the romance with the strongest positive feeling should be 'The Story of the Unknown Church', for in this Morris's feelings for nature and for mediaeval architecture both find an attractive outlet. The story is sad : the narrator is a master-mason who lives long enough to produce a monument for his dearest friend, Amyot, and his sister Margaret, and is finally found dead with his chisel in his hand, still after twenty years beautifying the tomb. The pathos of this is counterbalanced by the beauty of the church and its setting, as described in the early part of the story. Morris goes into considerable detail, especially over the carving of the west front, with the figure of Abraham in the Last Judgement. If the effect is pictorial rather than narrative, it is certainly effective. But there is a strong feeling, which we might associate with a reading of Ruskin, that this kind of beauty is part of a vanished world. From the beginning Morris has a strong sense of how human beings *ought* to live in a beautiful world, *ought* to create for themselves such a world, but the overall sadness of the story suggests that this hope is likely often to be frustrated. A sense of beauty and a sense of crisis are equally marked in these strange, imaginative stories.

In pursuance of his ambition to become an architect, Morris had entered the office of G. E. Street in Oxford in January 1856. Street was one of the best Victorian architects of the Gothic revival, as can be seen in such churches as St James the Less, Thorndike Street, Westminster and St Saviour's, Eastbourne, and his belief that the architect should also have an all-round knowledge of the crafts contributing to the interior decoration of his buildings must have been congenial to Morris. But he may have had reservations about Street's wholesale restoration of Oxford churches, and he found difficulty in making the detailed drawings of the doorway of St Augustine's, Canterbury, which constituted his main, less than inspiring, task in the office. However, it was there that he met Philip Webb, who was to become a successful architect after leaving Street's office in 1859, and one of Morris's life-long friends and co-workers.[9] By now Burne-Jones was living in London, attempting, with the encouragement of Rossetti, to become a painter. Morris met Rossetti on visits to London, and fell completely under the spell of his charismatic personality. Rossetti encouraged Morris, too, to paint, and Morris tried with his usual seriousness to master the medium. When Street moved his offices to London in the summer, Morris tried to combine the activities. In a letter in July he wrote:

> Rossetti says I ought to paint, he says I shall be able; now as he is a very great man, and speaks with authority and not as the scribes, I *must* try. I don't hope much, I must say, yet will try my best – he gave me practical advice on the subject . . . So I am going to try, not giving up architecture, but trying if it is possible to get six hours a day for drawing beside office work . . . I can't enter into politico-social subjects with any interest, for on the whole I see things are in a muddle, and I have no power or vocation to set them right in ever so little a degree. My work is the embodiment of dreams in one form or another.

At this stage Morris saw his vocation as exclusively artistic; later he was to find himself led back inexorably into a consideration of 'politico-social subjects' by the logic of his own artistic activities. Although he worked hard at painting – cancelling his articles with Street in the autumn to do so and abandoning the call of architecture as commercially practised – Morris did not achieve great success. The only existing painting by Morris is of Jane Burden in 1858, known originally as 'Queen Guenevere' and later as 'La Belle Iseult', and now in the Tate Gallery. The drawing of the figure is stiff, but the dress and patterned embroidery and carpet show Morris's feeling for colour and design. Other creative activities seemed more suited to his abilities – he tried carving, illuminating and embroidery, and designed some furniture for the rooms at 18 Red Lion Square recommended by Rossetti, into which he and Burne-Jones moved in November 1856. The great settle he had made by a carpenter, although so big that it could hardly be got into the room, is a splendid piece – it is now at Red House, Bexleyheath, though without the panels painted on it by Rossetti. Morris began pattern-designing, and his decorative ability also found expression in his work at the Oxford Union debating hall (now the

Old Library) in the long vacation of 1857. The opportunity to do this was given by the architect, Benjamin Woodward, a friend of Rossetti; a group of young enthusiasts led by Rossetti arrived to decorate the bays of the gallery in the octagonal hall with a series of scenes from Malory's *Morte D'Arthur*. The work was vastly enjoyable, but the results soon faded because of technical ineptitude. Morris's painting, of Sir Palomydes, was apparently undistinguished, while his decoration of the roof struck Ruskin as 'clever but not right'. (The restored ceiling now visible is a delicate and beautiful design by Morris carried out in 1875.)[10]

It was in Oxford at this time that Morris met Jane Burden, the 'stunner' who was to become his wife and the frequent and adored subject of Rossetti's later paintings. Rossetti was then living with his model, Elizabeth Siddal, whom he was to marry in 1860. He evidently encouraged Jane to accept the reticent and awkward Morris, with a mixture of motives at which we can only guess and which should therefore not be interpreted without sympathy. Rossetti was keen to keep together a group of friends, and there is no reason to suppose that he could foresee what might happen to them all after Lizzie's terrible suicide in 1862.

Morris had impressed his friends at Oxford by the unexpected power and originality of his poetry, and in 1858 he published the poems he had written over the previous few years, in *The Defence of Guenevere and other poems*. The title poem exemplifies the co-presence of the sense of beauty and the sense of crisis that had been characteristic of the earlier prose romances. In it Morris vigorously dramatises the crisis of the great love-story of Guenevere and Lancelot, as the Queen defies her accusers and throws aside the well-meant suggestion of Gawaine that her being with Lancelot was no proof of adultery. The poem opens with the Queen speaking, defending herself with a kind of reckless courage. The *terza rima* verse form is used with great skill, giving a steadying effect to what remains a tremendous outburst of indignation and romantic passion. Guenevere calls her beauty as evidence for her defence :

> Will you dare,
> When you have looked a little on my brow,

13

To say this thing is vile? or will you care
For any plausible lies of cunning woof,
When you can see my face with no lie there

For ever? am I not a gracious proof –

Guenevere dares the knights to condemn her, and we feel in the rhythms of the poetry her courage and determination. The ending of the poem, with the arrival of Lancelot 'at good need', completes the romantic pattern, but there remains the disturbing fact of Guenevere's marriage to Arthur to cast an ironic light on the depth of her passion for Lancelot. The poem is dramatic and vivid, a quickly glimpsed episode which re-animates the world of Malory without idealisation or spurious romance. That it embodies no fixed moral point of view is shown by the different perspective offered in the next poem in the volume.

'King Arthur's Tomb' is in alternately rhyming quatrains which carry the story along with some energy. Lancelot makes his way to Glastonbury where he is seeking Guenevere. He rides through the night with his mind full of memories of their love, which are given in a way that suggests both the cost of that love and the longing which survives. He reaches Glastonbury and makes his way to 'A place of apple-trees, by the thorn-tree / Wherefrom St Joseph in the days past preached'. Exhausted, he lays his head on a tomb, which he does not know to be that of Arthur. Guenevere's maidens inform her that Lancelot has arrived, and she goes to meet him, in a sombre mood and robed in black. She has been discomposed by a dream in which her love was associated with guilt – 'the grey downs bare / Grew into lumps of sin for Guenevere'. The awkward word 'lumps' makes the experience undignified, unromantic, merely negative. Guenevere awakens and prays for God's pardon, but is still unwilling to renounce Lancelot. Her distress is conveyed in the urgent, choppy rhythm of the poetry :

'If even I go to hell, I cannot choose
        But love you, Christ, yea, though I cannot keep
From loving Lancelot! O Christ! must I lose
        my own heart's love? see, though I cannot weep,

Yet I am very sorry for my sin . . .'

She is interrupted by the maid with the news of Lancelot's arrival, and goes at once to him, only to upbraid and reproach him for their infidelity to Arthur. Even in the reproach, however, Guenevere's lingering passion can be felt, as she dwells with fascination over memories of their love :

> 'Why were you more fair
>
> Than aspens in the autumn at their best?
> Why did you fill all lands with your great fame,
> So that Breuse even, as he rode, fear'd lest
> At turning of the way your shield should flame?'

Her sufferings in being prevented by passion from living the 'righteous life' which part of her nature wanted are poignantly conveyed, with the references to the 'tittering whispers' of the maids surrounding the isolated beauty of their queen. Even in chapel she had been obsessed by 'Lancelot's red-golden hair', thinking of him in the glorious world of male chivalry. Lancelot accepts her upbraiding with dignity, but she goes on to taunt him as a knight faithless to Arthur, 'a crooked sword' :

> 'Banner, and sword, and shield, you dare not pray to die,
> Lest you meet Arthur in the other world
> And, knowing who you are, he pass you by,
> Taking short turns that he may watch you curl'd
>
> Body and face and limbs in agony,
> Lest he weep presently and go away,
> Saying, "I loved him once" with a sad sigh –
> Now I have slain him, lord, let me go too, I pray.'
>
> *(Launcelot falls)*

Guenevere rushes off in desperation : she has done her duty, but it has only brought bewilderment and despair. But Lancelot is not dead : he awakens, and speaks the final verse :

> 'I stretch'd my hands towards her and fell down,
> How long I lay in swoon I cannot tell :
> My head and hands were bleeding from a stone,
> When I rose up, also I heard a bell.'

The bell suggests death, as if Guenevere has succumbed physically to her spiritual sacrifice. The main feeling conveyed is of the power of their mutual passion, and the sadness of a world in which it could not flourish naturally. No one is blamed, but the nature of things seems inexorably bleak.

This is true of most of the poems in the volume, whether they derive their subjects from Malory, as here, or from Froissart's account of the wars in France in the fourteenth century, or directly from Morris's imagination. The Froissartian poems recreate successfully an atmosphere of violence in which chivalry is a high ideal only occasionally achieved. Again, there is no idealisation of the fourteenth century, though there is respect for the few heroic figures who uphold the chivalric code. Fine poems of this type are 'Sir Peter Harpdon's End', 'Concerning Geffray Teste Noire', 'The Eve of Crecy', 'The Judgement of God' and 'The Haystack in the Floods'. This poem uses the octosyllabic couplet, but without the brashness often associated with that form. The movement is of sombre recognition of fact. The situation is dramatically developed from the unexplained question with which the poem opens :

> Had she come all the way for this,
> To part at last without a kiss?
> Yea, had she borne the dirt and rain
> That her own eyes might see him slain
> Beside the haystack in the floods?

The figures are at first anonymous, and the bleak atmosphere is dominant. Gradually the story reveals itself; we see the girl Jehane and her knight Robert stopped in their journey by Godmar and his thirty men. Morris does not exaggerate the scale; the numbers are small. Neither does he exaggerate the heroism of the participants. When Robert calls his men to attack the more numerous enemy with a reference to the Battle of Poitiers ('tis scarcely two to one'), his cry of 'St George for Marny !' is ignored, he is ignominiously caught about the neck by a kerchief, and made prisoner. And there is nothing chivalric about his enemy, Godmar. He wants Jehane and will kill Robert unless she gives herself to him :

'No'
She said, and turn'd her head away,
As there were nothing else to say,
And everything were settled . . .

Godmar then threatens to expose Jehane as a witch to the people of Paris, but she still refuses. The poem moves rapidly to its violent conclusion :

She saw him bend
Back Robert's head; she saw him send
The thin steel down; the blow told well,
Right backwards the knight Robert fell,
And moan'd as dogs do, being half dead . . .

·Romance ends in violence and disaster, as Godmar orders the now distracted Jehane back to his castle. The final couplet is now resonant with bleak intensity :

This was the parting that they had
Beside the haystack in the floods.

In poems like these Morris certainly re-animates the life of the Middle Ages, but he does not idealise it. The sense of beauty is almost overwhelmed by the sense of crisis.

Another poem that illustrates this forcefully is 'Concerning Geffray Teste Noire'. Froissart records the defence of his castle at Ventadour by this Breton freebooter. Morris's poem, however, uses its source very freely. The ballad-like quatrains are put into the mouth of John of Newcastle, sent by the Duke of Berry in the force of Sir John Bonne Lance to subdue Geffray, and now in old age recalling the past. Morris gives a dramatic effect by having John directly addressing a shadowy auditor called Alleyne :

Your brother was slain there? I mind me now
    A right good man-at-arms, God pardon him!
I think twas Geffray smote him on the brow
    With some spiked axe, and while he tottered, dim

17

About the eyes, the spear of Alleyne Roux
    Slipped through his camaille and his throat; well, well!
Alleyne is paid now; your name Alleyne too?
    Mary, how strange – but this tale would I tell –

(Morris's admiration for Browning can be felt in the rough but effective versification here.) John tells of how Bonne Lance, finding Geffray a difficult foe, eventually planned to trap him in the wood of Verville. The centre of the poem, however, is not the ambush but a discovery made while preparing it – that of two skeletons. By now the poem is in John's quoted speech, having moved from reminiscence to dramatic presentation. He notes details of the two skeletons, one small with no armour on the legs, the other a good deal larger. Aldovrand, evidently one of John's followers, suggests that the smaller is that of a woman. His question 'Didst ever see a woman's bones, my lord?' takes the poem a stage further back into itself with John's memories of entering Beauvais as a boy of 15 helping to put down the Jacquerie and 'smelling the burnt bones', who had fainted in response to his father's call to 'Count the dames' skeletons'. With nothing but a pair of dashes to mark the transition, the poem returns to the two skeletons, and John suddenly understands what has happened:

    Then I saw
The reason why she had on that war-coat,
    Their story came out clear without a flaw;

For when he knew that they were being waylaid
    He threw it over her, yea, hood and all;
Whereby he was much hacked, while they were stay'd
    By those their murderers; many an one did fall

Beneath his arm, no doubt, so that he clear'd
    Their circle, bore his death-wound out of it;
But as they rode, some archer, least afear'd
    Drew a strong bow, and thereby she was hit.

Still as he rode he knew not she was dead,
    Thought her but fainted from her broken wrist,
He bound with his great leathern belt – she bled?
    Who knows! he bled too, neither was there miss'd

> The beating of her heart, his heart beat well
>> For both of them, till here, within this wood,
> He died scarce sorry; easy this to tell;
>> After these years the flowers forget their blood.

This beautiful final line draws attention to the 'suns' of the primroses in the 'soft green moss', 'glimmering' beside the bones. The narrator recalls how he, who had previously been unable to bring himself to look at a skeleton, had 'pored for hours' over these, and come to see the dead lady herself :

> With her dear gentle walking leading in
>> By a chain of silver twined about her wrists,
> Her loving knight, mounted and arm'd to win
>> Great honour for her, fighting in the lists.

At this point the narrator addresses a lady – 'O most pale face . . . Your face must haunt me always', and asks if she is not suffering from some inward pain. The reader is bound to find this strange. Presumably the explanation is that John had 'raised' from the skeleton a vision of the lady as an object of desire :

> And when you talk your lips do arch and move
>> In such wise that a language new I know
> Beside their sound; they quiver, too, with love
>> When you are standing silent; know this, too,
>
> I saw you kissing once, like a curved sword
>> That bites with all its edge, did your lips lie,
> Curled gently, slowly, long time could afford
>> For caught-up breathings : like a dying sigh
>
> They gather'd up their lines and went away,
>> And still kept twitching with a sort of smile,
> As likely to be weeping presently –
>> Your hands too – how I watched them all the while!

This erotic reverie is broken by the voice of Aldovrand – 'Cry out Sir Peter now' – and the attack takes place. The enemy are killed, but Geffray is not after all among them : 'Months after that he died at last in bed / From a wound picked up at a barrier-fray'. This is the story that Alleyne is to tell to the Canon

of Chimay – Froissart himself – if he meets him in Ortaise. Thus,
by a witty irony, it might get written into Morris's sourcebook.
The poem ends, however, in a characteristic way for Morris :

> In my new castle, down beside the Eure,
>   There is a little chapel of squared stone,
> Painted inside and out; in green nook pure
>   There did I lay them, every wearied bone;

> And over it they lay, with stone-white hands
>   Clasped fast together, hair made bright with gold.
> This Jaques Picard, known through many lands,
>   Wrought cunningly; he's dead now – I am old.

Thus the lovers receive the kind of memorial Morris feels that
they deserve. The poem is typical in several ways. Most obviously,
it shows how naturally Morris's imagination moved in Froissart's
world, leaping from suggestion to suggestion with no sense of
effort (though the effect at a first reading is less than clear).
Then there is the respect for courage and loyalty, as seen in the
dead knight, set against the realistic observation of the world
of Geffray himself, in which cunning and violence survive for a
good while. And finally there is the intense feeling of the narrator
for the imaginary lady. The physical details (the mouth, lips,
kissing, with the strange simile 'like a curved sword / That bites
with all its edge') certainly give a vividness, which is very different
from realism, and justify the term erotic. The feeling of doomed
love implied here is strongly felt in many other poems of the
volume. It may be appropriate to look for a psychological
explanation of this in the young Morris's confused sexual feelings.
In the poetry, the result is powerful, strange and disturbing.

Other poems less directly concerned with Froissart's France
still evoke the turbulent world of the later Middle Ages; of these
'A Good Knight in Prison' and 'Riding Together' are particularly
effective. 'Shameful Death' suggests the tough world of the
border ballads, and 'Welland Rider' is a good ballad of a more
romantic kind. The longer narrative poem 'Golden Wings' also
belongs to the chivalric world, but it moves inexorably away
from the beautiful mood in which it opens :

On the bricks the green moss grew,
    Yellow lichen on the stone;
    Over which red apples shone;
Little war that castle knew.

Deep green water fill'd the moat,
    Each side had a red-brick lip,
    Green and mossy with the drip
Of dew and rain; there was a boat

Of carved wood, with hangings green
    About the stern; it was great bliss
    For lovers to sit there and kiss
In the hot summer noons, not seen.

This is idyllic, and painted with a vividness of colour which suggests Morris's affinity with Pre-Raphaelite painting. But once again the narrative refuses to leave the reader in the beautiful world. The figures we first see are moving in happy couples against the bright background, but then 'Fair Jehane de castel beau' is seen, alone. Sustained by love, she sings alone in her room to the knight whose return she is eagerly awaiting, but her song evokes no reply:

    Gold wings, the short night slips,
    The white swan's long neck drips,
    I pray thee, kiss my lips,
    Gold wings across the sea.

    No answer through the moonlit night;
    No answer in the cold grey dawn;
    No answer when the shaven lawn
Grew green, and all the roses bright.

The change from the flowing song to the regressive rhymes of the quatrain enacts Jehane's disappointment. In her despair she goes off to seek her knight, but when she is seen again it is as a dead body. The castle is now under attack, and its idyllic beauty is rapidly destroyed. The poem ends in a sombre reversal of its opening:

    The apples now grow green and sour
    Upon the mouldering castle-wall,
    Before they ripen there they fall:
There are no banners on the tower.

> The draggled swans most eagerly eat
> The green weed trailing in the moat;
> Inside the rotting leaky boat
> You see a slain man's stiffened feet.

The pattern of defeated love is again poignantly drawn.

'Golden Wings', like many other of these poems, is atmospheric and suggestive rather than very clear in the narrative, but in most cases this increases the reader's involvement. Some of the less historically-based poems in the volume are even less clear, and aroused the hostility of some early readers and the enthusiasm of others. These poems, which include 'The Wind', 'The Blue Closet' and 'The Tune of Seven Towers' (Morris had bought water-colours by Rossetti which provided starting-points for these two), 'Rapunzel', 'The Sailing of the Sword', 'Spell-Bound', and 'Near Avalon', are distinguished by their strange, remote atmosphere. 'The Wind' is perhaps the finest of the group; certainly it contains the most surreal moments:

> If I move my chair it will scream; and the orange will roll
> out far,
> And the faint yellow juice will ooze out like blood from a
> wizard's jar;
> And the dogs will howl for those who went last month to the
> war.
> > *Wind, wind! thou art sad, art thou kind?*
> > *Wind, wind, unhappy! thou art blind,*
> > *Yet still thou wanderest the lily-seed to find.*

This is a highly original poem, using the chorus to add to the sense of disturbing fantasy. We can discern vestiges of a story, as the narrator remembers the past; as in the other poems, the subject-matter is of love, violence and disaster. It is a nightmare poem which we can hardly explain but which imposes its strange vision upon the reader.

One contemporary critic who succeeded in conveying an acute sense of the atmosphere of these poems was the young Walter Pater. In a review of 1868 in the *Westminster Review* Pater looked back to Morris's first volume as having embodied the 'profounder mediaevalism' of Victor Hugo in France and Heine in Germany, by contrast with the earlier and more superficial mediaevalism of Scott and Goethe:

Of the things of nature the mediaeval mind had a deep sense; but its sense of them was not objective, no real escape to the world without one. The aspects and notions of nature only reinforced its prevailing mood, and were in conspiracy with one's own brain against one. A single sentiment invaded the world; everything was infused with a motive drawn from the soul.

This intense subjectivity is what animates Morris's poems, so that the mediaeval settings are not merely background; the mediaevalism is indeed profound. Some readers recognised this. When the first series of Tennyson's *Idylls of the King* was published in the following year, J. H. Shorthouse contrasted his treatment of the stories with Morris's, claiming that 'if the Arthurian Romances are ever to be worthily rewritten in modern poetry, it will be as Morris has done it, and not otherwise'. But it was Tennyson's blander treatment, with its greater emphasis on a moral pattern and example, which was to be popular with the Victorians.

A few contemporary readers appreciated *The Defence of Guenevere*. Ruskin in a letter to the Brownings called the poems 'most noble – very, very great indeed – in their own peculiar way' – a way, incidentally, that critics have felt to resemble that of Robert Browning himself. Swinburne, who had met Morris at Oxford, was enthusiastic, as was Rossetti, to whom the volume was dedicated. The reviewers, however, were few and they mostly found the poems difficult. When John Skelton submitted an appreciative review to the editor of *Fraser's Magazine,* John Parker, he was told, 'You ought really to say more as to Morris's obscurity and affectation'. Neither Dante Gabriel Rossetti nor his sister Christina had yet published a volume of poetry, so that Morris tended to be charged with the faults of all the Pre-Raphaelites as the reviewers saw them. H. F. Chorley in *The Athenaeum* felt that he 'must call attention' to this 'book of Pre-Raphaelite minstrelsy as to a curiosity which shows how far affectation may mislead an earnest man towards the fog-land of Art'. The *Spectator* felt that 'faults of affectation and bad taste seem too deeply seated' for Morris's poetic power to be likely to achieve anything of value. *The Saturday Review* saw Morris as 'the pre-Raphaelite poet' whose 'considerable powers' were 'altogether spoiled and wasted by his devotion to a false principle of art'. *The Ecclesiastic and Theologian,* however, welcomed the volume as representing the work of one of those 'no doubt laying the firm foundation for an honest and *bona fide* English school', though it regretted 'his want of precision and manifest obscurity'.[11] Nevertheless, Richard Garnett in *The Literary Gazette* and J. H. Pollen in *The Tablet* were favourable, and the poems became something of a cult among undergraduates in the next decade. Andrew Lang recorded in 1882 that he and several of his contemporaries at college in the 1860s, before the publication of *Jason,* knew *The Defence* almost by heart :

> We found in the earlier book something which no other contemporary poet possessed in the same measure; an unrivalled sense of what was most exquisite and rare in the life of the Middle Ages. We found Froissart's people alive again in Mr Morris's poems, and we knew better what thoughts and emotions lay in the secret of their hearts, than we could learn from the bright superficial pages of Froissart. In Mr Morris's poems the splendour of the Middle Ages, its gold and steel, its curiousness in armour and martial gear, lived again, and its inner sadness, doubt, and wonder, its fantastic passions, were re-born.[12]

George Saintsbury recorded a similar early experience of these poems when he looked back in his book of *Corrected Impressions* in 1895 :

> But I remember when . . . I bought the little brown book – nightingale-colour – from Slatter and Rose's counter at Oxford for a price which would not buy it now, that I took it back to my rooms and read it straight through with an ecstasy of relish not surpassed by anything I have ever known of the kind. Persons of sober and classical tastes fought very shy of 'Guenevere' at her first appearance . . . For my part I loved the book at once with a love full-grown and ardent; nor do I think that that love has decreased an inch in stature or a degree in heat since.[13]

24

With amusement Saintsbury noted that the poems, especially those like 'The Blue Closet' and 'Two Red Roses across the Moon', had 'the faculty of simply infuriating the grave and precise'.

The slightly younger J. Comyns Carr also remembered reading *The Defence* at about the same time with enthusiasm:

> I found there, though in a form perhaps deliberately archaic, that deeper note of passion which Tennyson's poetry, even at its best, deliberately lacks; and its appeal was the more urgent because Morris too was attracted by the charm of mediaeval romance – romance which in Tennyson's hands had lost some of its primitive dramatic quality, and became, as he developed the Arthurian story, more and more material for setting forth a systematised body of ethical teaching. Morris at a single stroke seemed to restore the legend to its historical place, and to recapture a part of its passionate significance.

But that the readership of *The Defence* was small is attested not only by our knowledge of the sales but by such retrospective comments as those of H. M. Hyndman in his *Record of an Adventurous Life* (1911). Hyndman, later to be associated with Morris in the early socialist movement, was a man of wide interests, and he found it hard to account for the fact that he did not come to know Morris's poems until several years after being 'swept away' by Swinburne's *Atalanta in Calydon* (1865):

> Yet it was not until Swinburne spoke of him as a great poet [in his review in the *Fortnightly Review* for July 1867] that the majority even of reading men were aware that so fine a genius was living unappreciated among us.
>
> He was much better known for his persistent revolutionary assaults upon the commonplace domestic decoration and furniture of the mid-Victorian period than for his delightful verse.

It is clear that as far as popular opinion was concerned Morris's early poems were largely unknown – only about 250 copies of the volume were sold. This helps to account for the fact that Morris, who had by now fallen in love with Jane Burden, the 'stunner' whom he married in 1859, failed to complete his next poetic undertaking, a series of poems on the fall of Troy. Instead he begun his 'revolutionary assault' on the decorative arts of his time, stimulated by the need to furnish the Red House, which was built for him by Philip Webb, to begin his married life. In so doing Morris was to reveal a talent for design worthy of the mediaeval craftsman he so admired. But *The Defence of Guenevere* remains for the modern reader as vivid evidence of potentialities in Morris which he did not fully develop in the art of poetry, and as one of the most original and striking single volumes of the age.[14]

2

The Firm and Poetry,
1860–70

At this time the revival of Gothic architecture was
making great progress in England and naturally
touched the Pre-Raphaelite movement also; I threw
myself into these movements with all my heart : got a
friend to build me a house very mediaeval in spirit in
which I lived for five years, and set myself to decorating
it; we found, I and my friend the architect especially,
that all the minor arts were in a state of complete
degradation especially in England, and accordingly in
1861 with the conceited courage of a young man I set
myself to reforming all that : and started a sort of firm
for producing decorative articles. D. G. Rossetti, Ford
Madox Brown, Burne-Jones, and P. Webb the architect
of my house were the chief members of it as far as
designing went. Burne-Jones was beginning to have a
reputation at that time; he did a great many designs
for us for stained glass, and entered very heartily into
the matter; and we made some progress before long,
though we were naturally much ridiculed. I took the
matter up as a business and began in the teeth of
difficulties not easy to imagine to make some money in
it : about ten years ago the firm broke up, leaving me

the only partner, though I still receive help and designs
from P. Webb and Burne-Jones.

. . . and then after a lapse of some years conceived
the idea of my *Earthly Paradise* and fell to work very
hard at it. I had about this time extended my historical
reading by falling in with translations from the old
Norse literature, and found it a good corrective to the
maundering side of mediaevalism. In 1866 (I think) I
published the *Life and Death of Jason,* which, originally intended for one of the tales of the *Earthly
Paradise,* had got too long for the purpose. To my
surprise the book was very well received both by
reviewers and the public, who were kinder still to my
next work, *The Earthly Paradise,* the first series of
which I published in 1868.

Morris was wealthy enough to be able to commission his friend
Philip Webb to design a house for him and Janey. A site was
found in an orchard at Upton in Kent, and the Morrises were
able to move into Red House (named after the colour of the
brick used) in the summer of 1860. Here were spent five happy
years, during which the two daughters were born. There were
many visitors, mainly old Oxford friends, and their recollections
stress the geniality which reigned within the house, often taking
the favourite Victorian form of practical jokes – of which Morris
was usually the victim. The house itself was built in the style
being evolved by architects like Street and Butterfield for
vicarages and schools – one which combined such Gothic features
as the high-pitched roof and the arches over the windows with
modern guttering, down-pipes and building materials. It stood
in a pleasant relationship to the garden, with a well dug to
provide the water and housed in a cone-roofed well-house within
the L-shape. (The house has recently been restored and brought
back into family use by Mr and Mrs Edward Hollamby).[1]
Inside, the oak staircase with its turret-shaped posts and
decorated ceiling is particularly effective. Morris decided to have
most of the furniture specially made – and the giant settle
brought along from Red Lion Square – so low was the quality
of the goods being produced at the time, when technical progress
had outstripped the sense of design. Friends contributed in

various ways – Webb designed furniture, candlesticks and table-glass, Rossetti painted a panel of the settle, Burne-Jones decorated the drawing-room with Arthurian scenes, while Morris designed wall-hangings and embroidery panels which Janey and lady visitors worked.

By this time both Rossetti and Burne-Jones had also married; Georgiana Burne-Jones was to become Morris's best woman friend. Her biography of her husband is an attractive book, and in it she recalls the happiness of early visits to Red House :

> It was not a large house, as I have said, but purpose and proportion had been so skilfully observed in its design as to arrange for all reasonable demands and leave an impression of ample space everywhere. It stood facing a little west of north, but the longest line of the building had a sunny frontage of west by south, and beneath its windows stretched a bowling alley where the men used to play when work was over . . .
>
> The deep porches that Edward mentions were at the front and the back of the house; the one at the back was practically a small garden-room. There was a solid table in it, painted red, and fixed to the wall was a bench where we sat and talked or looked out into the well-court, of which two sides were formed by the house and the other two by a tall rose-trellis. This little court with its beautiful high-roofed brick well in the centre summed up the feeling of the whole place.[2]

It is always interesting to relate writers and artists to their homes, but it is particularly significant in Morris's case, since he was a man with a marked sense of the importance of environment and its influence on human life. Red House is significant in the history of English vernacular architecture because of the contrast it presents to the ostentation and pretentiousness of much Victorian building; within it Morris was able, temporarily at least, to make a stand against the age.

And the building of the house had more positive results. Because of the dearth of well-designed furnishings available at the time, Morris and his friends found themselves developing the idea, originally suggested in a casual spirit, of establishing a commercial firm to manufacture goods of the required quality. From these discussions emerged the firm of Morris, Marshall, Faulkner & Company, which was to become a major influence on the development of design in many areas.[3] The Firm was officially opened in April 1861, with premises at 8 Red Lion Square. It consisted of Morris, Rossetti, Burne-Jones, Webb, Charles Faulkner, an Oxford friend, Ford Madox Brown, the artist and designer, and P. P. Marshall, a surveyor. Each partner put up £20 as capital by January 1862, and Morris's mother lent £100. Morris was to be paid £150 p.a. as manager, and Faulkner the same sum as book-keeper. Members were to be paid for work done. George Campfield, a glass painter, was taken on as foreman. The prospectus, probably written by Rossetti, described the Firm as 'Fine Art Workmen in Painting, Carving, Furniture, and the Metals'. Rossetti, Brown and Burne-Jones had already designed stained glass for Powells of White-friars, and this proved one of the most successful branches of the business. It is ironical that Morris and Burne-Jones, who had both abandoned the idea of a religious vocation, should find themselves devoting much energy to providing for the decoration of churches, as encouraged by the High Church movement. The architect G. F. Bodley provided two of the earliest commissions, at St Martin's, Scarborough, and St Michael's, Brighton. In the Exhibition of 1862 the Firm won two medals, and exhibited glass, furniture and hangings embroidered from Morris's designs. Table-glass, jewellery, tiles and wallpapers were also among the goods produced by this small but vigorous Firm.

In design Morris began to find the satisfaction that had eluded him in painting. Working in two dimensions he rapidly achieved authority and confidence. The first wallpapers were rather simple and naturalistic, but showed considerable charm. In designing them Morris showed no awareness of the more austere taste which had led the best designers of the previous decade, like Pugin and Owen Jones (author of the influential *Grammar of Ornament*, 1856), to emphasise two-dimensional formalism. By contrast, Morris's 'Daisy', 'Fruit' (or 'Pomegranate') and 'Trellis' all exhibit a marked degree of naturalism. They are also much simpler in form than Morris's later papers. All the papers were printed by Melford Warner of Jeffrey & Company. Morris was extremely meticulous about the quality of work produced from his designs, and took over the manufacture himself in all the other areas; he must have been satisfied with the quality achieved in the production of the papers, a comparatively simple process. (After the closing of Jeffrey & Company in 1930, the blocks were acquired by Sandersons, who were responsible for bringing Morris papers and chintzes back on to the market in the 1960s, with great success. Thus it is that many people today are familiar with Morris patterns when they know nothing of his other activities.)

However, at this stage Morris was devoting much of his energy to stained glass.[4] This art form was one of the splendours of the Middle Ages, as so many cathedrals and parish churches still fortunately show. It had fallen to a low level in the seventeenth and eighteenth centuries, when it came to be assumed that a window was simply a kind of painting. A striking and deplorable example of this known to Morris was the west window of New College Chapel, Oxford, adapted by Sir Joshua Reynolds from a painting by Correggio, 'La Notte', and made by Thomas Jervais in 1777–83. Opaque enamels were used for the colouring, since good quality coloured glass was unobtainable. The result was awkward and totally without the vitality which is so marked a feature of good mediaeval glass. An improvement in the quality of the glass occurred in the nineteenth century, due largely to the efforts of Charles Winston, whose influential *An Inquiry into the Difference of Style observable in Ancient Glass Painting* (1847) advocated the 'mosaic enamel method', employing separate pieces of glass for each colour where possible. Winston also went on to more practical measures of chemical experimentation, and as a result the firm of Powell & Sons of Whitefriars were able in 1856 to make several distinct colours in glass of good quality. (It was for Powells that Burne-Jones made his earliest designs.) With the establishment of the Firm, Morris was able to build on these foundations. In the early years, designs came from five hands, those of Rossetti, Burne-Jones, Madox Brown, Webb and Morris himself. At first Webb seems to have been responsible for the overall structures, but gradually this became Morris's responsibility. Although he was never very confident at drawing the human figure, Morris produced

31

satisfactory designs for early commissions like The Three Maries at the Sepulchre, the south aisle east window of St Michael and All Angels, Brighton (1862); The Tree of Jesse, the west window of St Stephen's, St Peter Port, Guernsey (1864); and the archangels Raphael, Michael and Gabriel, the south aisle window of St Mary's, King's Walden, Hertfordshire (1869). But his main contribution was made less in this way than in the flair he showed for translating the designs of others into suitable colours for the medium, inserting structurally conceived leading, and providing foliage backgrounds and decorative quarries.

Fortunately a good deal of Morris & Company stained glass can still be seen in different parts of England. The four panels 'King René's Honeymoon' (1862), now at the Victoria and Albert Museum, show the differing styles of Rossetti, Madox Brown and Burne-Jones, and serve as a reminder that the Firm provided glass for domestic as well as ecclesiastical purposes. But the finest achievements of the period were in some of the work done for the new churches, especially the large-scale work in All Saints, Middleton Cheney, Northamptonshire (1864–5), St Mary's, Bloxham, Oxfordshire (1869) and Holy Trinity, Meole Brace, Shropshire (1870). These show a successful combination of vitality in the individual designs – in the case of the earliest church, from no less than five artists – and an overall control which skilfully balances horizontal and vertical movement. For this, Morris can take the credit, as also for the colouring of these windows – and for the striking orange and gold of the trumpeting angels by Burne-Jones at St Edward the Confessor, Cheddleton, Staffordshire (1869). It is on the strength of such work that A. C. Sewter, the leading modern expert on Morris's glass, has written of his having 'a mastery of composition, and an understanding of the possibilities and necessary limitations of stained glass, which enabled him to create masterpieces once more in a medium which had produced scarcely any for centuries'.[5] A good example of Morris's own early work is The Annunciation in the tracery at Middleton Cheney, illustration no. 5. However, the Firm went on producing stained glass until its closure in 1940, so that a good deal of what may be seen today was produced after Morris's death and would not necessarily have gained his approval. But stained glass was one of the Firm's most important products, and they were fortunate in having contact with architects like G. F. Bodley who made frequent use of their work.

In 1862 other capital was raised to extend the Firm's range of activities, which came to include weaving and printing on cloth, and Morris was able to devote all his energies to these undertakings. Life at Red House was full of enjoyment, and it was planned to bring the Burne-Joneses to live in an extension. But in 1864 Morris fell ill, and also found himself in financial difficulties as the value of the shares left to him by his father declined. In 1865 he sold Red House, which he had regarded with so much affection that he could never bear to return there. He bought large premises at 26 Queen Square, Bloomsbury, where home and business could be under one roof. The elimination of the daily journey gave Morris more time for his own work, and the appointment of Warington Taylor as business manager, also in 1865, helped to increase efficiency. Morris had taken over the business affairs of the Firm from Faulkner, but had no great patience or interest in such matters. Taylor was a cultured man who had been unsuccessful in a varied career, and was employed at the time as a check-taker at the Opera House in the Haymarket. He soon proved himself an asset to the Firm, though Morris found difficulty in adjusting to his more businesslike outlook. It was thanks to Taylor that the Firm got on to the firm financial footing which was the basis of Morris's own subsequent security.[6]

The Firm was successful in obtaining some important non-ecclesiastical commissions in its early years. The first of these was for the redecoration of the Armoury and Tapestry Rooms in St James's Palace. This commission came from the First Commissioner of Public Works, William Cowper (later Lord Mount-Temple).[7] Cowper and his wife were friends of Ruskin, through whom they probably met Rossetti in 1865. Lady Mount-Temple's *Memorials* (1890) records the impact of Rossetti, and incidentally suggests the prevailing taste against which the Firm was struggling:

> You remember our dear little house in Curzon Street; when we furnished it, nothing would please us but watered paper on the walls, garlands of roses tied with blue bows! Glazed chintzes with bunches of roses, so

natural they looked, I thought, as if they had just been
gathered (between you and me, I still think it was very
pretty), and most lovely ornaments we had in perfect
harmony, gilt pelicans or swans or candlesticks,
Minton's imitation of Sèvres, and gilt bows everywhere.
One day Mr Rossetti was dining alone with us, and
instead of admiring my room and decorations, as I
expected, he evidently could hardly sit at ease with
them. I began then to ask him if it were *possible* to
suggest improvements! 'Well', he said, frankly, 'I
should begin by burning everything you have got.'

Lady Mount-Temple comments on the debt owed to the Firm
for having saved people 'from trampling roses underfoot, and
sitting on shepherdesses, on birds and butterflies, from vulgar
ornaments and other atrocities in taste, and for having their
homes homely and beautiful'. She also records with pleasure
that when the rooms at the Palace needed decorating, her
husband 'persuaded that great Reformer in Art, William Morris,
to undertake the work', rather than a fashionable upholsterer.
Philip Webb seems to have been responsible for the overall
scheme, with Morris supplying many of the details. Warington
Taylor's letters to Webb show his insistence on being businesslike;
in December 1866 he was exhorting Webb to charge proper
prices: 'Just remember we are embezzling the public money now
– what business has any place to be decorated at all?' – highly
un-Victorian sentiments. The work was completed in January
1867, and would seem to have been well regarded – so that the
Firm received further commissions for work at the Palace in 1880
and 1881. Some of the work is still to be seen, though not in
its original positions. It showed that the Firm had then confidence
to tackle public commissions and bring them off in suitable style.

Soon after this, in 1867, came the decoration of the Green
Dining Room at the South Kensington (now the Victoria and
Albert) Museum. The room contains two windows, with six
Burne-Jones panels in them of figures robed in white forming
a horizontal band. The walls are lined with green-painted panels,
with an ornamented row at eye-height consisting of sprays of
trees and flowers interspersed with figures representing the
months designed by Burne-Jones. Above the panelling is a foliage

34

design in raised and coloured plaster, and round the top is a frieze by Philip Webb of a chase of animals. Although the room had a public function, there is certainly an air of distinction and simplicity about it which must have impressed visitors. William Michael Rossetti, Dante's brother, noted a visit in his diary for 19 April 1870: '. . . the Refreshment-room painted by Morris: I think it must be the best piece of room-decoration, or something very like it, of the century, whether in England or elsewhere. It is darker than I like – i.e. the room admits less light: but I fancy this depends upon its position, not decoration.'[8] By now the room has lost its function and itself become an exhibit, and visitors can judge from its recently renewed colouring the validity of Rossetti's view. It is a little sombre for modern taste, though still impressive and uncluttered.

But such public commissions were naturally less frequent than those for private houses, sometimes brought about by personal contacts. To this period belongs the Firm's early work for Walter Bagehot, the lawyer and constitutionalist, whose 'fine taste', according to his biographer Mrs Russell Barrington, 'easily discerned in this work a distinguished quality which would be lastingly satisfactory'. Accordingly, the Bagehots' family home at Herd's Hill was altered and redecorated :

> We drove in from The Poplars to choose these papers in Morris's original premises in Queen's Square, Bloomsbury. The moral severity with which these prophets treated decoration and all matters of taste was not at that time quite understood in the rural districts of Somerset. The few smart houses near Herd's Hill were still decorated by second-hand French designs and white and gold ornament. Relations and neighbours were puzzled by Walter's choice. They were inclined to think Morris papers and furniture too plain and 'rather queer'.[9]

This again well suggests the background against which the Firm was operating. It was not the only source of good design at the time: the work of designers like Pugin, Owen Jones and Christopher Dresser deserves respect. But they worked as freelances, whereas the Firm could present new ideas – sometimes

35

less severely functional than those of Jones and Dresser – as part of a single recognisable strategy in the attack on Victorian middle-class taste, so often expressed in conspicuous consumption.

Morris travelled a good deal on the Firm's business, giving advice on decorative schemes wherever opportunities arose. A lively account of such an occasion is given in a letter of Lady Carlisle in 1870 :

> Morris arrived early this morning – with such a diminutive carpet-bag – He was rather shy – and so was I – I felt that he was taking an experimental plunge amongst 'barbarians' [the word recently used by Matthew Arnold in *Culture and Anarchy* to criticise the upper classes], and was not sure what would be the resulting opinion in his mind. However, he has grown more urbane – and even 3 hours has worked off much of our mutual shyness – A walk in the glen made me know him better and like him more than I fancied I should. He talks so clearly and seems to think so clearly that what seems paradox in Webb's mouth, in his seems convincing sense. He lacks sympathy and humanity, tho' – and this is a fearful lack to me – only his character is so fine and massive that one must admire – He is agreeable also – and does not snub me . . .
>
> The little Morris girls are delightful . . . and I could tell you amusing things about the little May who is such a materialist that she says 'the soul is nothing but the imaginary part of the body' – that there is nothing left but bones after death, that it is the brave that lives – She has not been taught these things, simply brought up without theology.[10]

It can be seen from this that Morris was impressive even to someone very aware of belonging to a different class; what Lady Carlyle felt as a lack of 'sympathy and humanity', despite his being 'agreeable', must have been Morris's intense absorption in the task in hand to the exclusion of much interest in the people concerned. The comments by and about the young May suggest how totally Morris lacked the concern for religion which marked so many of his contemporaries, though it clearly declined later in the century. It is a striking contrast with the agonising of such different thinkers as Darwin and Tennyson over the problems the idea of evolution offered to conventional belief. Morris's point of view was to be expressed succinctly in a conversation with the Irish poet William Allingham in 1882 when the subject was belief or disbelief in a God: 'he said "It's so unimportant, it seems to me", and he went on to say that all we can get to, do what we will, is a form of words'.[11] For Morris the question of religious belief was unimportant; there were so many urgent tasks to be undertaken in the struggle against the age that no time was left for speculation, whether philosophical or theological. Some reviewers of his poetry were to be troubled by this lack of religious concern.

An account of the Firm's shop is provided by Mrs C. W. Earle in her extremely popular book of social reminiscences, *Pot-Pourri from a Surrey Garden,* a book whose title suggests its unpretentious appeal to ladies of the middle class:

> The first time I went to Mr Morris's old shop in Queen's Square, quite as a girl, it was indeed a revelation. It had the effect of a sudden opening of a window in a dark room. All was revealed – the beauty of simplicity, the usefulness of form, the fascination of design, and the charm of delicate colour. Added to this came the appreciation of the things that had gone before, and which in my time had been hidden away. I came back to the various houses to which I had been accustomed with a sigh of despair; but the first step towards progress must always be discontent with what one has and with one's own ignorance.[12]

The terms of this description – especially 'the beauty of simplicity' – confirm the impression of how effectively the Firm's products as they became better known were presenting a challenge to the cluttered ostentation of so much interior design of the period.

Although Morris was much involved with work for the Firm in these years, he managed also to find time to write two of the longest and most popular poems of the age, *The Life and Death of Jason,* published in 1867, and *The Earthly Paradise,* 1868–70. His energy was truly formidable – the poems alone would seem sufficient achievement in themselves. There had been a gap in Morris's writing of poetry. After the publication of *The Defence of Guenevere* he had begun to write poems on the fall of Troy, but these dramatically conceived 'Scenes' were not completed or published. (They are to be found in Volume XXIV of the *Collected Works.*) They show some of the energy of the early Froissartian poems applied to the classical subject-matter, as in Paris's lament :

> 'But now – alas ! my honour is all gone
> And all the joy to fight that I had once
> Gone mouldy like the bravery of arms
> That lie six feet under the Trojan turf.
> Ah when I think of that same windy morn
> When the Greeks landed with the push of spears :
> The strange new look of those our enemies,
> The joyous clatter, hurry to and fro,
> And if a man fell it was scarce so sad –
> "God pity him" we said and "God bless him,
> He died well fighting in the open day" –
> Yea such an one was happy as I think,
> Now all has come to stabbing in the dark.'

From this it is reasonable to infer Morris's powerful though ill-defined sense of the complex problems of his own unheroic age, and it is greatly to be regretted that he did not complete the poem. But when he began writing again after leaving Red House, it was in a strikingly different manner, perhaps more manageable for a man who was busy in other fields simultaneously. He now planned a series of poems in which he could indulge his life-long love of narrative by bringing together many of the great stories from classical and mediaeval sources within a carefully conceived framework.

The story of Jason and the Golden Fleece was originally to have been part of the planned series, but Morris found it becoming too long for the scheme and decided to publish it on its own. *The Life and Death of Jason* appeared in June 1867 to encouraging reviews. Its seventeen books comprise some 1,000 lines of decasyllabic couplets, employed with great freedom, including much enjambement [over-running of the lines], in a manner derived from Chaucer. Although the subject is classical, the settings sound mediaeval, and the spirit is more pathetic than heroic. An early critic in the *Spectator* in June 1867 remarked perceptively that '*Jason* comes as near to *The Odyssey* as a poem written with Chaucer's strong sense of the piteousness of human life could come'. Towards the end, Morris directly invokes Chaucer, who is clearly the presiding influence on the poem :

> Would that I
>
> Had but some portion of that mastery
> That from the rose hung lanes of woody Kent
> Through these five hundred years such songs have sent
> To us, who, meshed within this smoky net
> Of unrejoicing labour, love them yet.
> And thou, O Master ! – Yea, my master still,
> Whatever feet have scaled Parnassus' hill
> Since like thy measures, clear, and sweet, and strong,
> Thames' stream scarce fettered bore the bream along
> Unto the bastioned bridge, his only chain.

In this we feel Morris's deep love of English landscape and the English past, and a suggestion of bitterness about the existing state of affairs in a world of 'unrejoicing labour'.

The narrative is evenly sustained throughout the long poem which tells the whole story of Jason's leading the Argonauts in search of the Golden Fleece, his success with the help of Medea, the killing of the usurper Pelias, his life with Medea and his marriage to Glauce and her death, and Jason's own death when his ship collapses upon him. Morris departs from his sources most in portraying Medea more as a loving woman than as a sorceress, and this enhances the pathos of the story. The poetry is easy to read, flowing on with a ready fluency, though rarely rising to dramatic force. Book 1 includes the speech of the usurped king Aeson to his son Jason, with its appealing vision of an Arcadian way of life :

> 'O child, I pray the Gods to spare thine head
> The burden of a crown; were it not good

That thou shouldst live and die within this wood
That clothes the feet of Pelion, knowing naught
Of all the things by foolish men so sought;
For there, no doubt, is everything man needs.
The quiver, with the iron-pointed reeds,
The carved bow, the wood-knife at the side,
The garments of the spotted leopard's hide,
The bed of bear-skin in the hollow hill,
The bath within the pool of some green rill . . .

And when the spring brings love, then mayst thou find
In some fair grassy place, the wood-nymphs kind,
And choose thy mate, and with her, hand in hand,
Go wandering through the blossoming sweet land;
And naught of evil shall there come to thee,
But like the golden age shall all things be;
And when upon thee falls the fated day,
Fearless and painless shalt thou pass away.'

This is characteristic of the poem in its straightforward, un-demandingly pleasant manner. But there is a kind of dramatic irony present for the reader, who knows already (if only from the synopsis at the beginning of the poem) that Jason's life will be quite unlike this, as he commits himself to action and adventure to reclaim his father's throne.

The poem includes a number of songs, in shorter, octosyllabic lines, which add variety and show Morris's lyrical powers. In Book 4 a water-nymph beguiles the 'fair-limbed Hylas', one of the mariners, in a song beginning :

I know a little garden close
Set thick with lily and red rose,
Where I would wander if I might
From dewy dawn to dewy night
And have one with me wandering.
And though within it no birds sing
And though no pillared house is there,
And though the apple boughs are bare
Of fruit and blossom, would to God
Her feet upon the green grass trod,
And I beheld them as before . . .

Hylas falls asleep, and 'the heedless sleeping man' is borne off by the nymphs and disappears into the river. Morris relates these incidents with an effective matter-of-factness, having achieved a convincing air of romance.

In Book 6 the travellers reach Aea, the land of King Aetes the usurper, whose 'marble house' is finely evoked :

> Silent it stood
> Brushed round by doves, though many a stream of blood
> Had trickled o'er its stones since it was built,
> But now, unconscious of all woe and guilt,
> It drank the sunlight that fair afternoon.

The elements of danger and outward beauty prefigure Jason's relationship with the apparently reasonable Aetes, who sets him a number of tasks which cannot in fact be achieved without supernatural aid. However, Jason receives such aid from Aetes's sorceress daughter, Medea, who has fallen in love with him. Medea's feelings are described as a 'honied pain', a romantic phrase reminiscent of Keats but suggestive of her future sufferings. For the moment, however, Jason is all gratitude and love :

> 'by this unseen delight
> Of thy fair body, may I rather burn,
> Nor may the flame die ever if I turn
> Back to my hollow ship, and leave thee here,
> Who in one moment are become so dear
> Thy limbs so longed-for, that at last I know
> Why men have been content to suffer woe
> Past telling, if the Gods but granted this,
> A little while such lips as thine to kiss,
> A little while to drink such deep delight.'

With Medea's aid Jason tames the brazen bulls and causes the Earth-born to destroy each other. Still the emphasis is on her love rather than on her sorcery, as in the scene at the beginning of Book 9 when she speaks presciently of Jason's being unfaithful to her, and prevents him from swearing his fidelity with loving words :

> 'Nay, sweet', she said, 'let be;
> Wert thou more fickle than the restless sea,
> Still should I love thee, knowing thee for such;

Whom I know not, indeed, but fear the touch
Of Fortune's hand when she beholds our bliss
And knows that nought is good to me but this.'

Morris always writes with particular tenderness at this period about the sufferings of love; the point will be taken up again in connection with *The Earthly Paradise,* where it is again obvious.

Now Medea beguiles the beast so that they can obtain the fleece, and Jason takes her away with him on the long return voyage. Orpheus's songs stand out against the background of the sustained narrative, expressing various moods. One in Book 10 is again of Arcadian innocence :

Alas ! for Saturn's days of gold,
Before the mountain men were bold
To dig up iron from the earth
Wherewith to slaughter health and mirth,
And bury hope far underground.
When all men needed did abound
In every land; nor must they toil,
Nor wear their lives in strife to foil
Each other's hands, for all was good
And no man knew the sight of blood.

Morris always kindled to such a vision of a happy, peaceful life, the contrast of which with human relations, whether of the nineteenth century or of the toiling mariners, creates its own poignancy. But Orpheus sings also in more vigorous tones, as in his defiant song 'O death, that makest life so sweet' in Book 12, looking forward to the reward the mariners will achieve when they reach their homes again. In Book 14 the Argonauts have to pass near the 'land of lies' to which the voices of the Sirens try to attract them. The Sirens' beguiling songs are, however, answered by Orpheus over some 300 lines of lyrical argument, and the mariners finally escape. This section bears comparison with Tennyson's 'The Lotos Eaters' (1842), in which, however, the mariners are beguiled and the poet himself seems to share their responses. Morris's Orpheus speaks for the human world of 'vine-coloured hillocks green' and sunburnt maidens, but it must be admitted that it is the Sirens' 'Come to the land where none grows old' which is more poetically eloquent. And in fact

Morris fails to achieve any great contrast of tone, partly because of the convention by which both contestants employ the same verse forms. Soon after this the weary mariners find themselves at the Garden of the Hesperides, another idyllic scene :

> Nor was there lacking many a living thing
> Changed of its nature, for the roe-deer there
> Walked fearless with the tiger, and the bear
> Rolled sleepily upon the fruit-strewn grass,
> Letting the coneys o'er his rough hide pass,
> With blinking eyes, that meant no treachery.
> Careless the partridge passed the red fox by;
> Untouched the serpent left the thrushes brown,
> And as a picture was the lion's frown.

Amidst the garden stands the apple-bearing tree, guarded by a dragon. The maidens sing lyrically of their 'green place' as a 'remnant of the days long gone', while the Argonauts take Medea's advice and sail on to seek their human fulfilment. This is achieved with the death of Pelias, brought about by the sorcery of Medea, who now summons Jason to reign : 'Come, conquering king, thy conqueror love to meet!' Thus Jason becomes king and the Argonauts disperse to their homes in Book 16. Book 17 brings the story from this felicity into disaster when, ten years later, Jason is persuaded by Creon into suspicion of Medea, and turns instead to Creon's daughter, Glauce. Spurned, Medea plans her revenge, sending a garment to Glauce which kills her on her wedding day. The scene is described through Jason's eyes :

> Giddy with joy one moment did he gaze
> And saw his love her slender fingers raise
> Unto the mantle's clasp – the next the hall
> Was filled with darting flames from wall to wall,
> And bitter screams rang out, as here and there,
> Scorched, as with outspread arms, the damsels fair
> Rushed through the hall, but swiftly Jason ran,
> Grown in one moment like an old worn man,
> Up to the dais, whence one bitter cry
> He heard of one in utmost agony,
> Calling upon his once so helpful name;

43

But when unto the fiery place he came,
Nought saw he but the flickering tongues of fire
That up the wall were climbing high and higher;
And on the floor a heap of ashes white,
The remnant of his once beloved delight,
For whom his ancient love he cast away,
And of her sire who brought about the day.

Although the event is dramatic, the telling lacks the energy of
the early Froissartian poems, and the line 'The remnant of his
once beloved delight' is an anti-climax – the word 'remnant'
seems inadequate to the scene. Nevertheless the poem proceeds
evenly to its conclusion with the death of Jason, and the funeral
games which accompany his being laid in 'a marble tomb carved
fair / With histories of his mighty deed' – as fitting an end
for a hero as Morris can conceive.

The Life and Death of Jason won for Morris the popularity
as a poet which *Guenevere* had signally failed to achieve. *Jason*
was initially published by Bell & Daldy at Morris's own expense,
but the bookseller F. S. Ellis advised Morris to seek a substantial
sum for the reprinting of the book in December 1867. Ellis then
took over the copyright, and also published *The Earthly Paradise*.
The early reviews show clearly what qualities were particularly
appreciated in *Jason* : clarity, picturesqueness, decorum, tenderness, reticence. Joseph Knight's review in the *Sunday Times* was
found by Morris himself an encouragement – he was naturally
relieved to receive better treatment than in 1858. Knight wrote :

> Its pictures are sharp, well-defined, and often of super-
> lative beauty. The poem is full of colour, not such rich
> and glowing hues as belong to the early volume, but
> wonderful colour nevertheless. Pale opal-like tints it
> exhibits . . . The melody of the versification is perfect.
> A frequent use of particular words adds to the dreary
> monotony which the author appears to have studied.

This may strike us as strange praise – 'dreary monotony' hardly
appears to us a desirable poetic quality. Knight goes on to note
that the poem is undramatic, 'destitute of fire and glow', but he
makes a saving comparison : 'It is as passionlessly beautiful as an

antique bust.' It would seem that the lack of dramatic force was willingly exchanged for the sustained quiet appeal of the poem's predominant tone. Henry James's account in the *North American Review* is along similar lines. James was only 24 at the time of the review, and his criteria are less demanding than those he was later to apply to fiction. Indeed, his conclusion suggests a limited view of what might be expected from poetry, which reflects a common assumption of the period :

> In spite of its length, the interest of the story never flags, and as a work of art it never ceases to be pure. To the jaded intellects of the present moment, distracted with the strife of creeds and the conflict of theories, it opens a glimpse into a world where they will be called upon neither to choose, to criticise, nor to believe, but simply to feel, to look, and to listen.

The appeal of the poem lay, that is to say, in its remoteness from the primary concerns of the age. James would certainly not have conceded later that a novel so restricted would be deserving of the highest praise. But in September 1867 he could give a correspondent, T. S. Perry, the advice : 'For real and exquisite pleasure read Morris's *Life and Death of Jason*. It is long but fascinating and replete with genuine beauty.'

Not that the poem escaped criticism altogether. Some reviewers regretted its excessive length, or its lax rhyming and versification, others the absence of drama and the changed characterisation of Medea. *The Athenaeum,* though basically favourable, ended with a reservation about Morris's philosophical position which meant that the poem's appeal was solely 'the presence of beauty' :

> Except in this respect, 'The Life and Death of Jason' has nothing in common with the hopes, the interests and the sympathies of modern life. For all that appears in the poem, the creed of Christendom might never have been professed. Its great lessons, that suffering ennobles, that self-sacrifice is the germ of blessedness, that man's earthly life is but a road, and death but a portal, to a more glorious realm, might never have been professed.

45

Whether the lack of religious or reasoning sentiment was due to Morris's respect for his material or to his own outlook could hardly be deduced from *Jason,* but it was to become a more significant issue with *The Earthly Paradise,* where it can be related more directly to the poet's own feelings.

Modern readers react to *Jason* in a way directly contrary to their Victorian predecessors. We find it hard to sustain interest in a long poem simply for the sake of the story, especially if that story is well known. Even *Paradise Lost* suffers from this change of attitude, despite its great rhetorical energy, and it may be doubted whether many readers complete *The Fairie Queene.* We are quite prepared for novels to be long and time-consuming, but the idea of devoting several evenings, say, to a poem like *Jason* is alien. Poetry, according to the modern belief which emerged with Yeats, Eliot and Pound, is essentially concise and usually lyrical; if you simply want stories, you may as well read prose. Despite the paradox that both Eliot and Pound wrote longer poems – Pound's *Cantos* indeed constituting one of the very longest – the assumption is still widely held and militates against much earlier poetry. If Jason's story can be told in a few pages of prose, we are disinclined to follow it through many pages of poetry. This is an undeniable fact, but in adopting this attitude we are depriving ourselves of pleasures which our fore-fathers clearly enjoyed. Even a sympathetic modern reader may conclude that *Jason* and Morris's other narrative poems are too long; but he will also discover many pleasures by the way, especially those associated with Morris's feeling for landscape and for the idyllic. He will not find the intensity and drama of some of the earlier poems.

The favourable reception of *Jason* encouraged Morris to go on with his projected series of stories drawn from a variety of sources and brought together in a neatly organised framework as *The Earthly Paradise.* A 'group of gentlemen and mariners of Norway' are envisaged in the fourteenth century, arriving in old age at 'some Western land' after a lifetime vainly spent in seeking an earthly paradise; here they are welcomed and settle, telling stories alternately with their hosts for every month of the year, beginning in March. The twenty-four stories so told constitute the bulk of the poem, though they vary considerably in length and form. The stories told, alternately classical and mediaeval, are roughly appropriate to the times at which they are narrated : those in March and April are mainly concerned with birth, youth and marriage; those from May to August deal idealistically with the quest for immortality in love, though this proves universally unsuccessful; those from September to November involve separation and death; and those from December to February exhibit a certain degree of resignation to experience. Yet in fact this pattern is much clearer to the retrospective critic than to the reader, who is more aware of a similarity of sombre mood in the poetry as he reads it.

The Earthly Paradise begins, however, with a carefully composed Apology, in which Morris puts forward very limited claims for what he is offering :

> Of Heaven or Hell I have no power to sing,
> I cannot ease the burden of your fears,
> Or make quick-coming death a little thing,
> Or bring again the pleasures of past years,
> Nor for my words shall ye forget your tears,
> Or hope again for all that I can say,
> The idle singer of an empty day . . .
>
> Dreamer of dreams, born out of my due time,
> Why should I strive to set the crooked straight?
> Let it suffice me that my murmuring rhyme
> Beats with light wing against the ivory gate,
> Telling a tale not too importunate
> To those who in the sleepy region stay,
> Lulled by the singer of an empty day.

Morris was frequently to be referred to in the terms which he applies to himself in this unusually introspective moment in the poem. We feel an unexpected sense of distress in this man who was usually so energetic in his response to life, as if some insoluble problem were imposing itself on his sensibility. Two kinds of explanation for this mood seem to offer themselves, one social, the other personal. The former is suggested by the opening lines of the poem proper :

> Forget six counties overhung with smoke,
> Forget the snorting steam and piston stroke,
> Forget the spreading of the hideous town;

Think rather of the pack-horse on the down
And dream of London, small, and white, and clean,
The clear Thames bordered by its gardens green;
Think, that below bridge the green lapping waves
Smite some few keels that bear Levantine staves,
Cut from the yew wood on the burnt-up hill,
And painted jars that Greek hands toiled to fill
And treasured scanty spice from some far sea,
Florence gold cloth, and Ypres napery,
And cloth of Bruges, and hogsheads of Guienne;
While nigh the thronged wharf Geffrey Chaucer's pen
Moves over bills of lading – mid such times
Shall dwell the hollow puppets of my rhymes.

This is a very frank introduction to the kind of poem which Morris is offering to his readers. It is an invitation to 'Forget', to 'Think rather', to 'Dream' of a beautiful past. The various attractive properties mentioned have become parts of bills of lading rather than of action – in contrast to the earlier poems where the descriptions were a part of the dramatic actions. And the phrase 'hollow puppets' would hardly apply to Guenevere or Sir Peter Harpdon, though it applies to some of the characters of *The Earthly Paradise*. Morris is stating his unequivocal distaste for his own times, and offering a poetry which will provide a more agreeable dream as an alternative to the reality. But in fact a strong undercurrent of sadness runs through the poetry too, as if the problem lay deeper – lay, that is to say, within human nature itself. The prevalence of unhappiness even within love, where happiness is chiefly sought, sounds sombrely through so many of the stories, and is taken up again in the more personal lyrical poems for each month which give variety to the structure. In these poems we sense a personal anguish which Morris reveals against the grain of his usual impersonal intention. This is most poignantly the case with 'November', in which the poet is struggling against an inner emptiness, the pull towards despair which concludes the first stanza :

Art thou so weary that no world there seems
Beyond these four walls, hung with pain and dreams?

The second stanza expresses the attempt to move beyond the self :

> Look out upon the real world, where the moon,
> Half-way 'twixt root and crown of these high trees,
> Turns the dead midnight into dreamy noon,
> Silent and full of wonders, for the breeze
> Died at the sunset, and no images,
> No hopes of day, are left in sky or earth –
> Is it not fair, and of most wondrous worth?

But the strangeness of the moonlit landscape undermines the hope of establishing contact with something positive. The suggestion that 'No hopes of day' survive seems to deprive the affirmative last line of much of its force – as if what is being affirmed is paradoxically evanescent. Thus one is prepared for the sadness of the final stanza:

> Yea, I have looked, and seen November there;
> The changeless seal of change it seemed to be,
> Fair death of things that, living once, were fair;
> Bright sign of loneliness too great for me,
> Strange image of the dread eternity,
> In whose void patience how can these have part,
> These outstretched feverish hands, this restless heart?

Here paradoxes are openly envisaged. The 'changeless seal of change' is seen in the November night with its bright moonlight that must give way to both darkness and dawn. Then the poet relates the scene again to himself. And far from having achieved comfort, the poet is even more desolate than at the beginning. He has roused himself into perception, but the perception itself is profoundly disturbing: the 'void patience' of 'the dread eternity' is no comfort to 'the restless heart' of man. The dialectical force of this is unusual in Morris's poetry, and makes this lyric one of the most memorable that he wrote. It could be construed – and this is indeed part of its value – as a protest against the limits imposed on man's life by the facts of the universe, by what is now described as man's alienation. But read within its context it reveals more personal significance, such as we surely find in a poem like 'May Grown A-Cold', published in *The Atlantic Monthly* in May 1870:

O certainly, no month this is but May!
Sweet earth and sky, sweet birds of happy song,
Do make thee happy now, and thou art strong,
And many a tear thy love shall wipe away
And make the dark night merrier than the day,
Straighten the crooked paths and right the wrong,
And tangle bliss so that it tarry long.
Go cry aloud the hope the heavens do say!

Nay, what is this? and wherefore lingerest thou?
Why sayest thou the sky is hard as stone?
Why sayest thou the thrushes sob and moan?
Why sayest thou the east tears bloom and bough?
Why seem the sons of man so hopeless now?
Thy love is gone, poor wretch, thou art alone!

The change from the reassuring romantic ideas of the first stanza
to the distress of the second is managed with unusual dramatic
force. For a man whose correspondence and behaviour show
a marked refusal of introspection, this is a revealing moment. We
can hardly fail to link it, and the whole spirit of *The Earthly
Paradise,* with a sense of the failure of Morris's marriage, and
his awareness that Janey was turning towards Rossetti. However
the whole affair is to be understood, there can be no doubt of
the suffering which it caused Morris in these years.

Morris was not, however, of a temperament to indulge his
distress passively, and at this time he began to develop a new
interest in Iceland and its culture. Morris met Eirikr Magnusson
in 1868, and with his help set about learning the language. From
the first he felt an intuitive sympathy with Icelandic literature
and history – a sympathy based on respect for the courage and
fortitude of a people making a life in such an inhospitable setting
as the frozen North. We can see this as part of a larger movement in Victorian culture to see England as part of northern
Europe rather than the south, which found expression at various
levels in such things as Kingsley's anti-Spanish sentiment in
Westward Ho!, the founding of the Early English Text Society
in 1864, R. C. Trench's *English Past and Present* of 1855 with
its discussion of 'English as it might have been' had there been
no Norman Conquest, and Gerard Manley Hopkins's use of
Teutonic diction. For Morris the appeal of the North was pro-

found, and it soon expressed itself in literary forms. In January 1869 'The Saga of Gunnlaug Worm-Tongue' appeared in *The Fortnightly Review,* to be followed in April by a translation of the Grettis Saga, and in May 1870 by The Story of the Volsungs and Niblungs from the Volsunga Saga. These supplemented the earlier translations of G. W. Dasent, which Morris knew, and helped to make the Icelandic stories available to the English reader. But the finest literary fruit of this new interest of Morris's was the story 'The Lovers of Gudrun' in the third part of *The Earthly Paradise,* derived from the Laxdaela Saga.

'The Lovers of Gudrun' is written in the rather casual couplet form which Morris derived from Chaucer. Morris keeps close to the central events of the saga in so far as they concern the tragic triangle of Gudrun, Kiartan and Bodli, beginning with Gudrun's dreams and their explication by Guest when he has seen the young Kiartan and his half-brother Bodli by the river. That scene is briefly given in the saga; in the Penguin translation by Magnusson and Palsson[13] it appears as :

> Gest looked at the young men for a while, and then told
> Olaf which one was Kjartan, and which Bolli, too, and then
> he pointed out with his spear-shaft each of the sons of
> Olaf and named by name all those who were there.

Morris renders the scene in great detail :

> Then toward the stream his spear-butt Olaf shook,
> As Steintor rose, and got somewhat aside,
> And showed the other twain he first did hide.
> On a grey stone anigh unto the stream
> Sat a tall youth whose golden head did gleam
> In the low sun; half covered was his breast,
> His right arm bare as yet, a sword did rest
> Upon his knees, and some half-foot of it
> He from the sheath had drawn; a man did sit
> Upon the grass before him; slim was he,
> Black-haired and tall, and looked up smilingly
> Into the other's face, with one hand laid
> Upon the sword-sheath nigh the broad grey blade
> And seemed as though he listened.

51

Critics have argued that in elaborating his saga material Morris was at times inclined to soften the effect by introducing Pre-Raphaelite descriptive detail,[14] but here Morris's rendering creates a memorable image of the two young men with the sword between them, pointing inexorably towards the tragedy. This is foreseen by Guest, who tells his son Thord :

> 'Thord, thou shalt live to hear when I am dead
> Of Bodli standing over Kiartan's head,
> His friend, his foster-brother, and his bane,
> That he in turn e'en such an end may gain.'

(Magnusson and Palsson : 'It will not surprise me if Bolli one day stands over Kjartan's body and earns his own death thereby; and that is a terrible thing to know about such fine young men.') Some of Morris's elaborations are most successful. For instance, his account of Kiartan, which suggests something of the quality of Yeats's tribute to Robert Gregory, 'soldier, scholar, horseman' :

> Fleet-foot, a swimmer strong, an archer good,
> Keen eyed to know the dark waves' changing moods,
> Sure on the crag, and with the sword so skilled
> That when he played therewith the air seemed filled
> With light of gleaming blades; therewith was he
> Of noble speech, though says not certainly
> My tale, that aught of his be left behind
> With rhyme and measure deftly intertwined;
> Well skilled was he, too, in the craftsman's lore
> To deal with iron mid the smithy's roar,
> And many a sword-blade knew his heavy hand.
> Shortly, if he amid ten kings should stand,
> All men would think him worthier man than they;
> And yet withal it was his daily way
> To be most gentle both of word and deed,
> And ever folk would seek him in their need,
> Nor was there any child but loved him well.

Kiartan leaves Gudrun, although they love one another, and goes to Norway with Bodli for three years. He is then kept by the King of Norway as a hostage for the conversion of Iceland to Christianity, and by the time this occurs and he is able to return, Bodli has persuaded Gudrun to marry him. Morris certainly plays up Kiartan's distress at the news by contrast with the saga's, 'He now heard about Gudrun's marriage and showed no sign of emotion at the news, although many people had been apprehensive about it'. Morris's Kiartan 'turned and staggered from the place, Crying aloud, 'O blind, O blind, O blind!'. This is no doubt extravagant, but one can recognise the difficulty posed for Morris by his hero's lack of emotion. It is all very well to say that the laconic force of the saga is what is impressive about it, but at this point we are not clear that Kiartan cares at all. Morris shows Kiartan recovering his self-control by a deliberate act of will, and eventually marrying the gentle Refna. But there is to be no lasting peace between the families. Gudrun is jealous of Refna and dissatisfied with Bodli, who eventually sets out with his followers to kill Kiartan. The scene is reported by 'a goodman of the dale' who sees Kiartan and his two followers accosted by Bodli with his eight. At first Bodli withholds himself from the fight, but finally Kiartan addresses him directly, and Bodli kills him. Again, Morris greatly elaborates the scene, but surely to good effect. The saga simply reads :

> Then Kjartan said to Bolli, 'It is an ignoble deed, kinsman, that you are about to do; but I would much rather accept death at your hands, cousin, than give you death at mine'.
>
> And with that, Kjartan threw down his weapons, and made no attempt to defend himself; he was only slightly wounded, but very weak with exhaustion.
>
> Bolli made no reply to Kjartan's words, but dealt him his death-blow all the same. Then Bolli caught him as he fell, and Kjartan died in Bolli's lap. At once Bolli repented bitterly of what he had done.

Anyone dramatising that scene would elaborate it, and 'dying words' are a literary convention which is widely accepted. This is Morris's version :

> And Bodli said, 'Wilt thou not then forgive?
> Think of the days I yet may have to live

Of hard life!'
        Therewith Kiartan oped his eyes,
And strove to turn about as if to rise,
And could not, but gazed hard on Bodli's face,
And gasped out, as his eyes began to glaze :

'Farewell, thou joyous life beneath the sun,
Thou foolish, wasted gift, – farewell, Gudrun!'
And then on Bodli's head back fell his head,
He strove to take his hand, and he was dead.

This cannot be considered long-winded, though its emphasis on the possibility of mutual forgiveness is not paralleled in the original. On the whole Morris rises to the challenge of the climax with strength and clarity.

Morris's handling of the conclusion is also effective in pointing up the saga without distorting it. Several years later, the son of Bodli and Gudrun asks his mother 'Which man did you love the most?' At first she simply describes the different qualities of her four husbands, but when pressed makes the gnomic statement 'I was worst to the one I loved the most'. The saga goes on :

'I think', said Bolli, 'that the truth has now been told.' And he said she had done right to tell him what he had been so curious to know.

    Gudrun grew to be very old, and people say she became blind. She died at Helgafell, and lies buried there.

Morris structures his conclusion so that the ending can be more emphatic :

She turned, until her sightless eyes did gaze
As though the wall, the hills, must melt away.
And show her Herdholt in the twilight grey;
She cried, with tremulous voice, and eyes grown wet
For the last time, whate'er should happen yet,
With hands stretched out for all that she had lost :

'I did the worst to him I loved the most.'

The effect is to focus the reader's attention on the strangeness and pitifulness of human life as crystallised in the story of Gudrun and her lovers. It brings out the implications by rearrangement, and shows Morris at his best in handling one of his most important sources.

Morris received a letter from his friend the poet Swinburne praising 'The Lovers of Gudrun' to which he replied – perhaps sensing an implied criticism – 'I am rather painfully conscious that the book would have done me more credit if there had been nothing in it but the Gudrun, though I don't think the others quite the worst things I have done. Yet they are all too long and flabby, damn it.' Modern readers may react in the same way, especially to the later stories, which are elaborated at greater length than those in the first sections of the poem. But this was not the typical Victorian reaction. For that we may quote a letter from Mary Howitt to Mrs Alfred Watts in March 1869 :

> I have vastly enjoyed Mr Morris's poems; and thus it is a pleasure to me to think of him in his blue blouse and with his earnest face at 'The Firm', and to feel that he is a great poet. I am glad that we had the fairy-tale tiles for the fireplace from Morris & Co.; their connection with this modern Chaucer gives them a new value and interest. Morris is not before Tennyson, but he stands very near him in the living reality of his old-world pictures, and in his exquisite painting of scenery; the flowers, the grasses, the 'brown birds', every individual object and feature in Nature is so lovingly and so faithfully portrayed. Tennyson's poetry is the perfection of art and truth in art. Morris's is Nature itself, rough at times, but quaint, fresh and dewy beyond anything I ever saw or felt in language. I shall try to tell Mr Morris what a joy and a refreshment it has been to me.[15]

This is a genuine if unsophisticated response to the poem; but readers vastly more intellectual like George Eliot and G. H. Lewes seem to have enjoyed it in much the same spirit. In a letter to the publisher John Blackwood from the Black Forest, he is told : 'We take Morris's poem into the woods with us and read it aloud, greedily, looking to see how much *more* there is in store for us. If *ever* you have an idle afternoon, bestow it on the *Earthly Paradise*.'

This was the general and favourable response which made the poem a great success. Sales were so high that a new contract was drawn up giving Morris a higher share of the profits; there were no fewer than five editions of the first volume between 1868 and 1870. Some reviewers expressed reservations, specially about what was felt to be the morbid philosophy underlying the poem. G. W. Cox in *The Edinburgh Review* in 1871 recognised the 'simplicity and grace' of the poems, but noted too that 'they carry with them the burden of a strange weariness and sadness', which he associated with their lack of spirituality : 'the music of this Earthly Paradise is mournful because it is so earthly'. Similarly *The Athenaeum* in 1870 complained of 'an ominous sound which is continually breaking in like the toll of a knell – death! death! death!' – inappropriate to the tenor of 'a book of fanciful tales'.[16] But the conclusion was hopeful : 'Mr Morris is still a young man and may live (we trust so) to repent of infusing into his fine Book of Tales so unwholesome an ingredient.' Not surprisingly, the reviewer of *The Christian Observer* in 1870 – who regretted that 'so little genuine poetry . . . is now proceeding from Evangelical men' – noted the lack of religious feeling and argued that the poem expressed 'the prevalent tone of feeling in the present day'.[17] This was not so much 'avowed infidelity' as 'the Epicurean indifference – which is, after all, man's true natural religion – which would fain make the most of the world, and over which the consciousness of a world to come does but cast a dark shadow and a chilling fear'.

A young reviewer in 1868 had noted the same characteristics but evaluated them very differently. This was Walter Pater, whose review in the *Westminster Review* in 1868 covered all Morris's poetry so far published. He noted :

> One characteristic of the pagan spirit these new poems have which is on their surface – the continual suggestion, pensive or passionate, of the shortness of life; this is contrasted with the bloom of the world and gives

new seductions to it; the sense of death and the desire
of beauty; the desire of beauty quickened by the sense
of death.

Pater then went on to argue that there is a distinct affinity
between this mood and the findings of 'modern philosophy'. This
philosophy, he suggested, emphasises the inconstancy of all
processes, the changefulness of both the outer and the inner
worlds which leaves the individual isolated and bewildered:
'Struggling, as he must, to save himself, it is himself that he loses
at every moment.' In the situation of feeling ourselves, after an
interval, condemned to death, Pater recommended that 'our
one chance is in expanding that interval, in getting as many
pulsations as possible into the given time'. Although such a
'quickened sense of life' may be derived from various sources
including 'political or religious enthusiasm, or the "enthusiasm
of humanity"', its most reliable source is art, 'for art comes to
you professing frankly to give nothing but the highest quality
of your moments as they pass, and simply for those moments'
sake'. This eloquent passage Pater later transferred to his book
The Renaissance (1873) as its conclusion, where it became a
powerful influence on the generation of Oscar Wilde and the
Nineties which saw art as a man's salvation, because of its purity
and separation from normal human concerns. Morris was also
to think deeply about the nature of art, but because he was so
involved in the applied arts his thinking was to take a different
direction, one deeply concerned with 'political enthusiasm' and
'the enthusiasm of humanity'.

The reviewers were right to sense in Morris's poetry at this
time a poignant undercurrent of unhappiness; he was looking
for a faith, though neither Christianity nor Pater's aestheticism
could provide it. He still needed to find a way of bringing his
feelings for the idyllic into a relationship with the realities of
his age. In *The Earthly Paradise* that sense appears only as an
aspiration, as in the beautiful song sung by Apollo when a herds-
man in Thessaly in 'The Love of Alcestis':

> O dwellers on the lovely earth,
> Why will ye break your rest and mirth
> To weary us with fruitless prayer;

Why will ye toil and take such care
For children's children yet unborn,
And garner store of strife and scorn
To gain a scarce-remembered name,
Cumbered with lies and soiled with shame?
And if the gods care not for you,
What is this folly ye must do
To win some mortal's feeble heart?
O fools! when each man plays a part,
And heeds his fellow little more
Than those blue waves that kiss the shore
Take heed of how the daisies grow.
O fools! and if ye could but know
How fair a world to you is given.

O brooder on the hills of heaven,
When for my sin thou drav'st me forth,
Hadst thou forgot what this was worth,
Thine own hand had made? The tears of men,
The death of threescore years and ten,
The trembling of the timorous race –
Had these things so bedimmed the place
Thine own hands made, thou couldst not know
To what a heaven the earth might grow
If fear beneath the earth were laid,
If hope failed not, nor love decayed.

This kind of plaintive aspiration found a ready response in a wide audience, for its romantic vagueness deprived it of any dangerous implications. The popularity of *The Earthly Paradise* was due largely to its providing an inoffensive pleasure to its middle-class readers, and the opportunity to turn away from current problems into a simpler world. Buxton Forman noted that 'These poems are such as no man need scruple to take home to his wife and leave within reach of his children'. Elizabeth Hasell's review in *Blackwood's Magazine* in 1869 saw Morris's mission as a relaxing one :

But when the hour for lotus-eating has come; when we stroll up the lane beneath its banks of honeysuckle or roses, or watch the 'tremolar della marina' from the beach; or when we light the lamp and draw the curtains after a hard day's work on some autumn evening, then comes the turn of the poet who is willing and able to amuse us. It is then that we seek for verse which can soothe the wearied mind with images of beauty, which can be enjoyed without effort, and which condescends to be entertaining.[18]

Similarly in 1870 the *Spectator* began its review of Part 3 with a question, the answer to which was provided by the poem :

Whither shall a reader turn in these days who longs to escape for a while from all the toil and clamour and strife of the world, and to roam at will in pleasant places, where nothing shall remind him of the doubtful battle-field where after a short breathing-space he must again bear his part?

In this sense the 35-year-old Morris seems very much in harmony with the needs of his age. He was spoken of as the peer of Tennyson, Browning and Matthew Arnold in poetry, and the work of the Firm was expanding. Yet, as we have seen, there were also hints in the poetry of a deep sense of frustration, of an awareness of the gap between the real and the idyllic, which were to drive Morris onward to explore new areas of thought and action, and leave behind 'the idle singer of an empty day'.

A vivid account of William and Janey Morris as they appeared at this time to a stranger is to be found in a letter from Henry James to his sister Alice in March 1869. The letter is written with exhilaration, conveying a strong sense of the personalities concerned; no doubt there is an element of entertaining exaggeration, but that is also the novelist's keenly observant eye at work :

But yesterday, my dear old sister, was my crowning day – seeing as how I spent the greater part of it in the house of Mr Wm Morris, Poet . . . Morris lives on the same premises as his shop, in Queen's Square, Blooms-bury, an antiquated ex-fashionable region, smelling strong of the last century, with a hoary effigy of Queen Anne in the middle. Morris's poetry, you see, is only his sub-trade. To begin with, he is a manufacturer of

stained glass windows, tiles, ecclesiastical and mediaeval
tapestry, altar-cloths, and in fine everything quaint,
archaic, Pre-Raphaelite – and I may add, exquisite.
Of course, his business is small and may be carried on
in his house : the things he makes are so handsome,
rich and expensive (besides being articles of the very
last luxury) that his *fabrique* can't be on a very large
scale. But everything he has and does is superb and
beautiful.

James then goes on to describe Janey :

> . . . she haunts me still. A figure cut out of a missal –
> out of one of Rossetti's or Hunt's pictures – to say this
> gives but a faint idea of her, because when such an
> image puts on flesh and blood, it is an apparition of
> fearful and wonderful intensity. It's hard to say
> whether she's a grand synthesis of all the Pre-
> Raphaelite pictures ever made – or they a 'keen
> analysis' of her – whether she's an original or a copy.
> In either case she is a wonder.

After dinner Morris read to the company from one of the
Bellerophon poems, amid 'the picturesque bric-a-brac of the
apartment' (hardly a description Morris would have liked) while
Janey nursed a toothache in silence. The description ends with
the poet :

> Morris himself is extremely pleasant and quite different
> from his wife. He impressed me most agreeably. He is
> short, burly, corpulent, very careless and unfinished in
> his dress . . . He has a very loud voice and a nervous
> restless manner and a perfectly unaffected and business-
> like address. His talk indeed is wonderfully to the point
> and remarkable for clear good sense. He said no one
> thing that I remember, but I was struck with the very
> good judgement shown in everything he uttered. He's
> an extraordinary example, in short, of a delicate
> sensitive genius and taste, saved by a perfectly healthy
> body and temper.

No wonder James found it 'a long rich sort of visit, with a strong peculiar flavour of its own'. Whatever his problems and perplexities, Morris was an impressive personality who would face up to them with courage, determination and 'clear good sense'.

3

Iceland and
Kelmscott Manor, 1871-7

In 1872 I published a fantastic little book chiefly
lyrical, called *Love is Enough*.

Meantime about 1870 I had made the acquaintance
of an Icelandic gentleman, Mr E. Magnusson, of whom
I learned to read the language of the North, and with
whom I studied most of the works of that literature;
the delightful freshness and independence of thought of
them, the air of freedom which breathes through them,
their worship of courage (the great virtue of the human
race), their utter unconventionality took my heart by
storm. I translated with Mr Magnusson's help, and
published, *The Story of Grettir the Strong*, a set of
Sagas (about six) under the title of *Northern Love
Stories*, and finally the Icelandic version of the *Niblung
Tale*, called the *Volsunga Saga*.

In 1871 I went to Iceland with Mr Magnusson,
and, apart from my pleasure in seeing that romantic
desert, I learned one lesson there, thoroughly I hope,
that the most grinding poverty is a trifling evil compared with the inequality of classes. In 1873 I went to
Iceland again. In 1876 I published a translation of the
Aeneid of Virgil, which was fairly well received. In

1877 I began my last poem, an Epic of the Niblung Story founded chiefly on the Icelandic version. I published this in 1878 under the title of *Sigurd the Volsung and the Fall of the Niblungs.*

Through all this time I have been working hard at my business, in which I have had a considerable success even from the commercial side; I believe that if I had yielded on a few points of principle I might have become a positively rich man; but even as it is I have nothing to complain of, although the last few years have been so slack in business.

Almost all the designs we use for surface decoration, wallpapers, textiles, and the like, I design myself. I have had to learn the theory and to some extent the practice of weaving, dyeing and textile printing : all of which I must admit has given me and still gives me a great deal of enjoyment.

In this account, Morris refers to his writings and the work of the Firm, as well as the appeal of Iceland, but is characteristically silent about his private life. The indications are, however, that it was an unhappy time for him with Janey finding in Rossetti qualities missing in her husband. By now their two daughters were growing up, and Morris was looking for a larger house away from London. When he found Kelmscott Manor in 1871, however, it was taken on a joint tenancy with Rossetti, as if Morris was still hoping that the situation could be controlled by goodwill. Lizzie Siddal had died in 1862, and after 1867 Rossetti and Janey appeared a good deal together in artistic society, he as lively, she as enigmatic as ever. Some of the sonnets in Rossetti's *House of Life* sequence express his returning vitality in her companionship. The facts of the case are hard to establish in detail, but it would seem that Janey had become Rossetti's mistress, though it is also likely that his feelings were more deeply engaged than hers.[1] Rossetti needed human support in proportion as his high claims for his art both in poetry and painting were matched with a consistent hesitancy to publish or exhibit the work and so submit it to possible criticism. When he was persuaded by his friends to publish his poems in 1870, he took every precaution to ensure favourable reviews, even getting the reluctant Morris to contribute a 'puff' to *The Academy*. This was all to no avail when in October 1871 Robert Buchanan crudely attacked the morality of Rossetti's poems in 'The Fleshly School of Poetry' in *The Contemporary Review;* the article included a witty side-blow at Rossetti's friends Morris and Swinburne :

> He cannot tell a pleasant story like Mr Morris, nor forge alliterative thunderbolts like Mr Swinburne. It must be conceded, nevertheless, that he is neither so glibly imitative as the one, not so transcendently super-ficial as the other.

For Rossetti the criticism came as deeply distressing, and he began to move away from his former friends into isolation and neurosis. Nevertheless, as his paintings show, it was the vision of Janey Morris's archetypal beauty which was one of his more enduring resources in his time of difficulty.

Kelmscott Manor was to be one of the great consolations of Morris's later life. It is a typical irregular Oxfordshire manor house, probably dating from the Elizabethan period but with many later additions, and having that organic relationship to its setting which was Morris's highest architectural value – and which Red House had, more deliberately, aimed at. The house stands in what is still a quiet part of the Thames valley, thirty miles by water from Oxford and some three miles from the little town of Lechlade. It is a gentle landscape, most of the villages enhanced by beautiful mediaeval churches and often by magnificent barns, like that at Great Coxwell, 150 feet long and regarded by Morris as one of England's great buildings. The pastures by the many small rivers of the area are well wooded, and Morris often noted in his letters the abundance of the bird-life; he also had the chance to indulge his passion for fishing. The untitled and uncompleted novel[2] which Morris wrote at this time (and which had been abandoned by 22 June 1872 when he sent the manuscript to Mrs Alfred Baldwin as 'a specimen of how not to do it') is clearly set in the Oxfordshire countryside. This is affectionately described, as in the opening description of the village :

Old as the village street was it looked still older, for in that country of good building stone, people kept on building all decent houses with little mullioned windows a good hundred years later than in most parts of England, and the houses here were mostly built of the brown stone with grey stone slate roofs.

A later description of Mr Mason's 'cool clean house with its sanded passages' is even more effective, as Morris writes of the

impression which clung to the whole house that though old, handsome in decoration and picturesque in outline, it had never been built for anything different from what it was : everything was what was thought fit for a rich farmer of that passed day, and everything added had grown on to the place as naturally as the growth of the big limes and walnuts.

Morris obviously felt himself less successful with the human side of the novel, which seems to have been concerned with the love of two young men for the same girl – a story with obvious biographical implications. Morris lacked the psychological interest, the readiness for self-exposure, which makes success in this mode possible, and rightly decided to express himself in other ways.

One of them was the writing of illuminated manuscripts, a craft which Morris had practised a little as an undergraduate inspired by the manuscripts in the Bodleian Library, but to which he now devoted a great deal more energy and attention – and with striking results.[3] The Gothic Revival had led in the mid-century to a renewed interest in mediaeval manuscripts, particularly by those wishing to illuminate passages from the Bible, and Morris's three known early manuscripts – his poem 'Guendolen' and a song from Browning's 'Paracelsus' in 1856, and the translation of the opening of Grimm's story 'Der Eisenhaus', probably in 1857 – are very much in the manner and spirit of the Middle Ages. When he began illuminating again as his Sunday occupation between 1869 and 1875, he produced some 1,500 pages in several styles of calligraphy. 'A Book of Verse', completed in August 1870, for Georgie Burne-Jones's birthday, shows a development from the early pages with powdered ornamentation to a more vital, organic style later on, with growth from the base of the rectangle filling the right side and often moving into the spaces between the stanzas; a poem from the book is shown in illustration no. 3. Morris's next gift to Georgie, 'Story of the Dwellers of Eyr', ran to 254 pages and is in a simple style. On the other hand, his version of 'The Rubaiyat of Omar Khayyam' only 6 inches high, is richly ornamented. A second 'Rubaiyat', for Burne-Jones, is similar though more restrained. For his fourth gift to Georgie, Morris chose three Icelandic sagas; 240 pages completed in February 1874, with a thicker nib producing emphatic strokes in both the lower case and the unusual capitals. Morris's two final manuscripts were of classical texts, *Odes* of Horace and Virgil's *Aeneid;* neither is complete. The *Odes* comprise a small volume in an italic hand, with large illuminated initials and crowds of gold discs with rays around them, giving a very rich decorative effect. The calligraphy was finished, but not the decoration of the 183 pages. The effect is a mixture of classical and mediaeval details. In the Virgil, however, begun in 1874 and worked on for over a year, the effect is more purely classical. A roman script is employed, well proportioned and dignified. The coloured capitals are not allowed to encroach on the text, and the result is a magnificent piece of craftsmanship. By 1875, however, Morris had abandoned the project, and he never returned to this form of art. Translating the *Aeneid* now took his attention, and the study of dyeing. But he had proved yet another aspect of his astonishing versatility, in a craft the practice of which could give pleasure only to a few friends. We can see in this his consistent attachment to an idea of the potential richness and beauty of life which set him at odds with his age's pride in its technological achievements.

Morris continued to write poetry during the period, though nothing he published was to rival the popularity of *The Earthly Paradise*. Some of the short poems appeared in the *Fortnightly Review*, but not in book form until *Poems by the Way* in 1892, and others were not published at all, perhaps because Morris felt them to be too personal. The most consistent source of inspiration was Iceland, which Morris visited for the first time on a very enjoyable visit with Magnusson, Charles Faulkner and a new friend, W. H. Evans in 1871. Morris recorded his impressions in vigorous straightforward prose in his *Journals,* not intended for publication.[4] The trip ended with the pleasant detail of Morris's bringing back his pony, Mouse, which was to become a great favourite of the girls at Kelmscott Manor. The poem 'Iceland First Seen' commemorates Morris's impression of the country whose mythology he already admired so much. It is written in a style derived from the verse-form of some of the Icelandic poetry he had translated, with none of the smoothness of his earlier versification :

> Lo from our loitering ship
> a new land at last to be seen;
> Toothed rocks down the side of the firth
> on the east guard a weary lea,
> And black slope the hillsides above,
> striped adown with their desolate green :

The poet goes on to ask what it is the travellers hope to see in this 'desolate strand', which is the place of 'the undying glory of dreams'. His imagination returns to the land associated with Brynhild and Balder :

> Ah! when thy Balder comes back
> and we gather the gains he hath won,
> Shall we not linger a little
> to talk of thy sweetness of old,
> Yea, turn back awhile to thy travail
> whence the Gods stood aloof to behold.

The 'travail' of Iceland represents something like the heroism which his imagination had sought to re-create in his early poetry but the possibility of which his own age seemed emphatically to deny.

However, Morris's most elaborate poem of this period, *Love is Enough,* published in 1872, has little that is Nordic about it, apart from the adopting of an unrhymed alliterative metre for the dramatic sections, which would seem to suggest knowledge on Morris's part of the mediaeval narrative poem *Piers Ploughman*. Morris employs a peculiarly complex form in this poem, for which no exact analogies can be produced. The Argument gives a succinct introductory account :

The story, which is told by way of a morality set before
an Emperor and Empress newly wedded, showeth of a
king whom nothing but Love might satisfy, who left all
to seek Love, and, having found it, found this also,
that he had enough, though he lacked all else.

The centre of the work is thus 'a morality', a play in the
mediaeval didactic mode. In accordance with this association,
Love is present as a character in various guises, as well as
speaking the prologue and epilogue to each scene. But Morris
complicates matters further by having two sets of 'frames' – the
peasant lovers Giles and Joan, who speak in octosyllabic couplets,
and the courtly lovers, the Emperor and Empress, who use
decasyllables. In addition, there are a number of lyrical passages
described as 'The Music', which consistently recur to the central
theme. The first of these sounds when the Emperor and his
consort enter :

> Love is enough : though the world be a-waning
> And the woods have no voice but the voice of complaining,
>   Though the sky be too dark for dim eyes to discover
> The gold-cups and daisies fair blooming thereunder,
> Though the hills be held shadows, and the sea a dark wonder,
>   And this day draw a veil over all deeds passed over,
> Yet their hands shall not tremble, their feet shall not falter,
> The void shall not weary, the fear shall not alter
>   These lips and these eyes of the loved and the lover.

This is a more elaborate form than Morris usually employed,
and it possesses the musical quality which is implied by the title.
But the flowing quality of the rhythm and syntax – all one
protracted sentence – have the effect of depriving the opening
assertion of any dramatic emphasis, and the overall effect of
the poem is similar. The initial dialogue between the Emperor
and Empress, with its balanced quatrains, promises more
authority than the later writing exemplifies. The tale of Pharamond excites little interest, since his search for Love is too
obviously expected to be crowned with success. Yet the management of the poem's elements shows considerable skill of a kind
not shown by Morris before : for instance, it is a neat device for

the Music to be brought nearer to the characters for the climactic moment of the discovery of the sleeping Pharamond by the beloved Azalais, and for the two characters to employ the rhythms typical of the Music for their affirmation of faith at the end of the scene :

KING PHARAMOND

Let us speak, love, together, some word of our story,
That our lips as they part may remember the glory.

AZALAIS

O Love, kiss me into silence lest no word avail me;
Stay my head with thy bosom lest breath and life fail me.

The simplicity of the couplets used by the peasant couple at the end brings out the sophistication of these earlier devices, and leads the poem pleasantly back into a less elevated, though still pastoral, world :

GILES

– Come, o'er much gold mine eyes have seen,
And long now for the pathway green,
And rose-hung ancient walls of grey
Yet warm with sunshine gone away.

JOAN

Yes, full fain would I rest thereby,
And watch the flickering martins fly
About the long eave-bottles red
And the clouds lessening overhead :
E'en now meseems the cows are come
Unto the grey gates of our home,
And low to hear the milking-pail :
The peacock spreads abroad his tail
Against the sun, as from the lane
The milkmaids pass the moveless wain . . .

Morris always responds, as both poet and designer, to the simple beauties of the countryside, which offered a haven to his imagination from the grimmer aspects of his age.

But for all these positive qualities, the lack of dramatic life at its centre is a major defect in *Love is Enough,* and may lead one to wonder how deeply Morris believed his own message. The language sometimes comes near to the religious, as in Love's account of his treatment of Pharamond :

> . . . Ye know me : I have sent
> A pain to pierce his last coat of content :
> Now must he tear the armour from his breast
> And cast aside all things that men deem best,
> And single-hearted for his longing strive
> That he at last may save his soul alive.

But his Love has no Christian overtones; it is purely human and, the plot emphasises, individualistic. It might seem that amid the uncertainties of his own private life, Morris was trying to endow Love with the power he would have liked it to possess rather than anything deeply experienced by him. In view of his growing sense of social responsibility, the treatment of the public issue is surprising. Pharamond is fated to follow Love and leave his country, and when he returns to it at the end, it is simply to leave again : 'Nay, one thing I have sought, I have sought and have found it.' The country to which he will return is 'The poor land and kingless of the shepherding people / There is peace there, and all things this land are unlike to.' The question of responsibility is not really faced. It is not surprising that the Mayor should apologise about this aspect of the play when he offers it to the Emperor, though the latter is able to draw his own moral from it, of the need to pass from 'kingcraft' to Love. It may seem unreasonable to press such questions in relation to a poem whose tone is far from intellectual; but it has to be said that *Love is Enough* can hardly sustain the didactic burden which Morris imposes upon it, though it is a work of considerable skill and charm. It was not finally by adopting an idealising stance that Morris was to find his answer to the problems of age. Where Pharamond is led by Love to 'tear the armour from his breast', Morris found it necessary to take on more of the warrior-stance of the Icelandic heroes.

A great deal of Morris's time and energy continued to be directed to the work of the Firm. In 1871 George Wardle became manager, and his powers of organisation were important in helping to increase its efficiency. Clients, both ecclesiastical and private, continued to come forward with large commissions, and the chintzes and wallpapers began to be used by a wider range of customers. By 1872 the premises in Queen Square had become too small to accommodate both the business and the Morris family, and a house was found in Turnham Green, where they lived for the next six years. It had the convenience of being not too far from the Burne-Joneses in Fulham, and the journey to Queen Square was reasonable. The Firm was now in possession of additional workshops and a better showroom, which helped the expansion of its business. However, this brought its own problems, because the amateurish organisation which had seemed reasonable in 1861 was no longer adequate for the efficient running of the established Firm – or so Morris came to believe. Of the original partners, Burne-Jones, Faulkner and Webb accepted the situation and refused financial compensation when Morris decided to reorganise the business under his own name alone. This was really a recognition of the actual state of affairs, for he was the only one whose livelihood largely depended on the Firm. But Rossetti, Madox Brown and Marshall insisted on their legal rights, and lengthy negotiations were necessary before the reconstitution as Morris & Company at the end of March 1875. Morris's relationship with Rossetti never recovered from the controversy, but the reconstituted Firm flourished.

Of the products of the Firm, stained glass continued to be very important. Morris was producing a decreasing amount of figure design, none at all after 1873, but his contribution in the form of decorative quarries and foliage backgrounds, together with his responsibility for the interpretation and colouring of the designs provided by Madox Brown and Burne-Jones, amounted to a highly significant one. A number of particularly important windows were produced, including those at Christ Church Cathedral, Oxford; Jesus College Chapel, Cambridge; Holy Trinity, Meole Brace, Shropshire; and All Hallows, Allerton, Liverpool. Meole Brace has windows of 1870 and 1871 by Madox Brown, and of 1871-2 and 1873 by Burne-Jones, as well as later glass by the Firm. The contrast between the work of the two designers is clearly represented here. The apse left window, mainly by Madox Brown, is a good deal more dramatic than the right window, by Burne-Jones. But the nine small scenes are perhaps too cramped to be altogether appropriate for dramatic treatment; the visitor may feel somewhat overwhelmed, and prefer the quieter manner of Burne-Jones. The windows in Christ Church also represent the work of several years: 1870–1; 1872–3; 1875, and 1878. The most impressive is the Vyner Memorial east window in the lady chapel, erected in memory of an undergraduate murdered by Greek brigands. This is a four-light window, with figures of Samuel, David, St John the Evangelist and Timothy, each with a small panel below. The main figures are in white patterned with gold, with deep blue backgrounds, and they provide the main areas of light. The dense foliage in the upper part of the window extends into the tracery, giving a richly decorative effect.

The way in which backgrounds of this type give emphasis to the main figures can also be seen in the Jesus College windows, dating from 1873 to 1878, and including designs by both Madox Brown and Burne-Jones. The chapel is an interesting example of the Firm's work, since it also contains painted ceilings of 1866–7 with angels holding scrolls, designed by Morris (finely restored in 1950), and wool tapestry curtains on the east wall and at the choir screen. There are also windows in the choir from designs by Pugin, the Roman Catholic architect who was one of Morris's inspirers. The rich colour of the windows leads to a dark interior, although the figures stand out well by virtue of their light colouring. Sunshine is needed to enable the visitor to enjoy the details of the backgrounds. The development of Burne-Jones's sense of overall pictorial composition, by contrast with the dramatic intensity of Madox Brown's smaller-scale work, can be seen in the fine east window of the chancel at Allerton, the River of Paradise. The five lights are here unified by the central image, that of the Lamb of God standing on rocky ground, with the four rivers flowing down in silver ribbons, while angels and the Blessed look up towards the Lamb from a landscape below. There is a fine sense of movement combined with overall structure, achieved partly by the delicacy of the colouring. The same church contains fine windows of the Evangelists (1876); Noah, Moses, Daniel and St Paul (1879); Miriam, Ruth, Esther and Mary (1880), all with especially rich foliage and fruit panels. The quality of these windows is brought out by contrast with less interesting work, also by the Firm, later in the 1880s, where colour is far less imaginatively employed.

Morris designed nine wallpapers between 1872 and 1876, and these show a marked change from his earlier naive designs. The best of them – 'Jasmine', 'Vine', 'Larkspur', 'Acanthus', 'Chrysanthemum' – give a remarkable sense of free movement within the overall unemphatic but lucid structure. As their names suggest, Morris's inspiration comes always from nature. He ignored the movement towards more abstract design deriving from the work of Pugin and Owen Jones and supported in books like Christopher Dresser's *Principles of Decorative Design* (1873). Morris bases his pattern and colours on nature, but shows his genius in the way in which these motifs become part of satisfying wholes. The range of density is considerable, from the delicacy of 'Jasmine' with its varied greens and tiny red dotted flowers to the richness of 'Acanthus', the subtle colour gradations of which required sixteen blocks for printing. The love of nature which found expression so often in the settings of his poems comes out with equal emphasis here, and supports Morris's view – which we may see as deriving from Romanticism – that the designer will be concerned not to invent novelties but to reveal the harmonies of nature. That these papers were becoming popular with the middle class is suggested by the enthusiasm of one of the characters in a sentimental American novel, Annie Hall Thomas's *Maud Mohun* of 1872. Her advice to a friend is to 'make your walls artistic without the aid of pictures', and this is to be done by turning to 'Morris Papers' with 'those wonderful greyish-blue backgrounds on which limes, lemons and pomegranates with their respective foliages intertwine luxuriantly. How eye-comforting and perfect they are in their wonderful admixture of grey and blue "undertone", on which blooming fruits repose, that look as if they were executed by Nature'.[5] Morris might have been embarrassed by the extravagance of this, but hardly by its central response.

From wallpapers to printed textiles was not a long step for Morris the designer to take, since both employ repeating patterns on a relatively small scale. His first design was 'Tulip and Willow' in 1873 (not successfully produced until 1883), followed by 'Honeysuckle', 'Marigold', 'Tulip', 'Iris', 'Larkspur', 'Carnation', 'African Marigold' and 'Bluebell' (1876). These are again stylised naturalistic designs with a good deal of vitality, consisting of simple elements. The earliest designs were printed by Thomas Clarkson of Bannister Hall, Preston, but although his block printing methods satisfied Morris, the chemical dyes he used did not. Morris was dissatisfied with the tone of the colours produced, and from 1875 employed Thomas Wardle (his manager's brother), whose works at Leek, Staffordshire, were noted for the quality of their silk dyeing. Morris developed his interest in dyeing with characteristic energy, reading all the available textbooks, and studying the great herbals like that of Gerard, which gave relevant information about plants. He began experimenting in a scullery at Queen Square, and later travelled regularly to Leek to study Wardle's experiments. It was important to Morris that the textiles sold by the Firm should be of the highest quality, and in order to achieve this he was prepared to work at the problems for as long as two or three years. He came to choose the most reliable of the commercial dyes available, and relate his colour schemes to what was possible in this way. He also learned the use of indigo and madder vats, which had by then become virtually obsolete. In 1876 he set up a small dye-house at Queen Square, and did all the Firm's dyeing himself. The result was that the public could become confident of the quality of colour in the fabrics offered for sale, and expect them to prove durable. Attention to these basics by Morris helps to account for the Firm's success as it aimed to extend its range of high-quality products available to the public.

These activities did not, however, exhaust Morris's energy. He also designed a number of Kidderminster, Wilton, Brussels and Axminster carpets, which were executed in the ordinary commercial way by outside firms, and were therefore not particularly expensive. And the embroidery work of the Firm also continued. Typical of this period is the 'Romance of the Rose' frieze which was designed by Morris and Burne-Jones for the dining-room of Sir Lowthian Bell's Rounton Grange, Northallerton, by Philip Webb. The tapestry was worked by Margaret Bell and her daughter Florence Johnson, and completed in 1880. The three panels, with their rich and dignified effect, may now be seen in the William Morris Gallery at Walthamstow. That Morris did not find that his work as a decorator fully satisfied his critical attitude towards the age is suggested by the anecdote of his once turning on Bell, a wealthy iron-maker, who had heard him walking about excitedly talking to himself and asked the reason, with the words 'It is only that I spend my life in ministering to the swinish luxury of the rich'.[6] He was becoming acutely aware of the limited market for the Firm's goods in the England of his time with its concentration of wealth in the hands of the few, although at this point he had not looked for a political explanation of the situation.

Morris's literary activities also continued unabated, at first mainly in the form of translations. He was still working at Icelandic with Magnusson, and he paid a second visit to Iceland in the summer of 1873, which he enjoyed much more than his only visit to Italy, with Burne-Jones, earlier in the same year. Morris's companions to Iceland this time were Faulkner and the archaeologist J. H. Middleton, whom they met on the boat. A more adventurous journey to the interior was undertaken and recorded in clear, factual prose in the *Journals*. Morris's response to the stark simplicity of the country was even deeper than before. The image of the land and the lives of endurance of its people suggested an alternative to Victorian industrial England which appealed deeply to Morris's imagination. The people of the island, it seemed to him, had a dignity and self-respect which were rapidly being destroyed in his own country by the profound and uncontrolled changes which were part of the Industrial Revolution. He could at least show his respect for Iceland by making some of its great stories available in English. Not surprisingly, he was doubtful whether Wagner's treatment of the Sigurd (or Siegfried) story in his series of operas, *The Ring*, could do justice to the greatness of the myth; to him opera seemed, as he put in a letter of 12 November 1873, 'the most rococo and degraded of all forms of art'. Wagner, with equal reverence for the myth and equal contempt for most contemporary opera, was in fact in the process of creating an adequate form for his powerful imagination, but Morris was not receptive enough to new styles of art to recognise this. By 1875 he had a number of translations by him, and these were brought together as *Three Northern Love Stories*, though three shorter tales were included alongside the three which provide the title: 'The Story of Gunnlaug the Worm-tongue', 'The Story of Frithiof the Bold' (both published originally in magazines) and

'The Story of Viglund the Fair'. The style employed by Morris and Magnusson is well exemplified by a passage from the first story :

> So one Saturday evening Helga sat in the fire-hall, and leaned her head upon her husband's knees and had the cloak, Gunnlaug's gift, sent for; and when the cloak came to her, she sat up and plucked at it, and gazed thereon a while, and then sank back upon her husband's bosom, and was dead. Then Thorkel sang this :—

> > Dead in mine arms she droopeth,
> > My dear-one, gold rings' bearer,
> > For God hath changed the life-days
> > Of this lady of the linen.
> > Weary pain hath pined her,
> > But unto me, the seeker
> > Of hoard of fishes highway,
> > Abiding here is wearier.

The aim is a directness and clarity of diction and syntax which will bring out the stark simplicity of the human situations which the stories embody.

In the same year, 1875, Morris published *The Aeneids of Virgil,* a full translation of Virgil's epic. This is further evidence of his extraordinary energy and versatility, as well as of his more than adequate classical scholarship, a seldom emphasised quality. The mixture of dignity and romantic pathos in *The Aeneid* makes the poem particularly hard to translate; Morris naturally emphasised the more romantic elements. He chose to use the fourteen-syllable couplets of Chapman's *Homer,* which certainly give a measured flow to the poem. Henry Nettleship's review in *The Academy* had the authority of a scholar who was to become Professor of Latin Literature at Oxford in 1878; Nettleship noted a few inaccuracies and a few infelicities, but claimed that 'we have found Mr Morris, as a rule, as careful in his renderings as he is scrupulous and delicate in his handling of metre and rhythm'. Few translations of well-known poems survive beyond the generation in which they are written, and Morris's is not known today. However, a comparison between his rendering of a descriptive passage in the first book with that by Cecil Day Lewis in 1952 is not entirely to Morris's disadvantage. Morris:

> There goes a long firth to the sea, made barren by an isle,
> Against whose sides thrust out abroad each wave the main doth
>   send
> Is broken, and must cleave itself through hollow lights to wend.
> Huge rocks in this hand and on that, twin horns of cliff, cast
>   dread
> On very heaven; and far and wide beneath each mighty head
> Hushed are the harmless waters; lo, the flickering wood above
> And wavering shadow cast adown by darksome hanging grove:
> In face whereof a cliff there is of rocks o'erhung, made meet
> With benches of the living stone, and spring of water sweet,
> The house of nymphs: a-riding there may way-worn ships be bold
> To lie without the hawser's strain or anchor's hooked hold.

Day Lewis:

> A spot there is in a deep inlet, a natural harbour
> Formed by an island's flanks upon which the swell from the
>   deep sea
> Breaks and dividing runs into the land's recesses.
> At either end of the lofty cliffs a peak towers up
> Formidably to heaven, and under these twin summits
> The bay lies still and sheltered: a curtain of overhanging
> Woods with their shifting light and shadow forms the backdrop;
> At the seaward foot of the cliffs there's a cave of stalactites,
> Fresh water within, and seats which nature has hewn from the
>   stone –
> A home of the nymphs. Here, then, tired ships could lie, and
>   need
> No cable nor the hooking teeth of an anchor to hold them.

The modern version is less obviously poetic; the intention is to give the reader a neutral version which will remind him of the original but not compete with it. Morris makes a far stronger impression, but not without strain. The long lines, indeed, hardly achieve the Virgilian sweetness, and sometimes appear clumsy. Yet at the end there is a sense of poetic energy which is likely to carry the reader onward, and this is a basic quality for a narrative poem. *The Aeneids* is not an unqualified success, but it is no disgrace to Morris as either poet or classicist.

However, Morris's great effort as poet and translator at this period was his version of the Icelandic *Volsunga Saga* published as *The Story of Sigurd and the Fall of the Niblungs* in 1876. The prose version which Morris wrote with Magnusson had appeared as long ago as 1870; now his imagination was able to play freely over the material which had become so familiar and significant to him, and produce a highly dramatic work. Morris employs couplets as in *The Aeneids,* but now the lines are even longer, hexameters which are basically iambic but include frequently substituted anapaests and dactyls, particularly in the first and fourth feet of each line. This gives a vigorous but unsubtle move-ment, and certainly carries the narrative on. Alliteration is used freely, but the diction is comparatively straightforward. (More archaisms had been employed in the prose version.) Morris made some modifications to the traditional story, in the light of the associated *Elder Edda* (as with the ring of fire round Brynhild on the mountain), and others to achieve greater verisimilitude. He very much wanted English readers to recognise the greatness of the saga, and softened it in some respects to achieve this. In particular, his treatment of love is more courtly and mediaeval than Icelandic. Odin's wrath is given greater prominence, probably in the interests of unity, and the ending is changed for this purpose too.

A brief summary of Morris's poem with quotations will make it possible to get some idea of his achievement. The first book 'Sigmund', is not directly concerned with Sigurd but with his father; it therefore stands somewhat aside from the rest of the narrative. But it is briskly narrated, and Morris's imagination responds splendidly to the challenge of describing the hall of the kings :

> Thus was the dwelling of Volsung, the King of the
>   Midworld's Mark,
> As a rose in the winter season, a candle in the dark;
> And as in all other matters 'twas all earthly houses' crown,
> And the least of its wall-hung shields was a battle-world's
>   renown,
> So therein withal was a marvel and a glorious thing to see,

For amidst of its midmost hall-floor sprang up a mighty tree,
That reared its blessings roof-ward, and wreathed the roof-tree
  dear
With the glory of the summer and the garland of the year.
I know not how they called it ere Volsung changed his life,
But his dawning of fair promise, and his noontide of the strife,
His eve of the battle-reaping and the garnering of his fame,
Have bred us many a story and named us many a name;
And when men tell of Volsung, they call that war-duke's tree,
That crowned stem, the Branstock; and so was it told unto
  me.

The second book, 'Regin', lives up to its splendid introductory
summary: 'Now is the First Book of the Life and Death of
Sigurd the Volsung, therein is told of the Birth of him, & of his
Dealings with Regin the Master of Masters, & of his Deeds
in the Waste Places of the Earth.' This book introduces the
accursed gold, the slaying of the serpent Fafnir and of Regin,
and the rescue of Brynhild. It ends with the couple's mutual
profession of love:

'I shall seek thee there', said Sigurd, 'when the day-spring is
  begun,
Ere we wend the world together in the season of the sun.'

'I shall bide thee there', said Brynhild, 'till the fulness of
  the days,
And the time for the glory appointed, and the springing-tide
  of praise.'

From his hand then draweth Sigurd Andvari's ancient Gold;
There is nought but the sky above them as the ring together
  they hold,
The shapen ancient token, that hath no change nor end,
No change, and no beginning, no flaw for God to mend:
Then Sigurd cried: 'O Brynhild, now hearken while I swear,
That the sun shall die in the heavens and the day no more
  be fair,
If I seek not love in Lymdale and the house that fostered
  thee,
And the land where thou awakedst 'twixt the woodland and
  the sea!'

79

And she cried : 'O Sigurd, Sigurd, now hearken while I
  swear,
That the day shall die for ever and the sun to blackness
  wear,
Ere I forgot thee, Sigurd, as I lie 'twixt wood and sea
In the little land of Lymdale and the house that fostered
  me !'

Then he set the ring on her finger and once, if ne'er again,
They kissed and clung together, and their hearts were full
  and fain.

In Book Three, 'Brynhild', the couple part again in Lymdale,
and Sigurd goes to the Niblungs.

At first Sigurd is successful in warfaring – the main activity
of the Niblungs. Then he is given the Cup of Evil to drink by
Grimhild the Wise Wife, and forgets his loyalty to Brynhild. He
marries the Niblung princess Gudrun, and later it is he who woos
Brynhild for King Gunnar, and wins her by a trick. Not surprisingly, there is 'Contention betwixt the Two Queens', and
eventually Sigurd is killed by Guttorm :

Close over the head of Sigurd the Wrath gleams wan and bare,
And the Niblung woman stirreth, and her brow is knit with fear:
But the king's closed eyes are hidden, loose lie his empty hands,
There is nought 'twixt the sword of the slayer and the Wonder
  of All Lands.
Then Guttorm laughed in his war-rage, and his sword leapt
  up on high,
As he sprang to the bed from the threshold and cried a
  wordless cry,
And with all the might of the Niblungs through Sigurd's body
  thrust,
And turned and fled from the chamber, and fell amid the dust,
Within the door and without it, the slayer slain by the slain;
For the cast of the sword of Sigurd had smitten his body atwain
While yet his cry of onset through the echoing chambers went.

The book ends with 'The Mighty Grief of Gudrun' and the
death of Brynhild :

'How then when the flames flare upward may I be left behind?
How then may the road he wendeth be hard for my feet to find?
How then in the gates of Valhall may the door of the gleaming
    ring
Clash to on the heel of Sigurd, as I follow on my king?'

The final lines are finely elegiac.

Book Four, 'Gudrun', takes us back to the violence of the
story of Sigurd, with the destruction of the Niblungs by King
Atli, who had married Gudrun, and with Gudrun's death:

Then Gudrun girded her raiment, on the edge of the steep
    she stood,
She looked o'er the shoreless water, and cried out o'er the
    measureless flood,
'O Sea, I stand before thee; and I who was Sigurd's wife!
By his brightness unforgotten I bid thee deliver my life
From the deed and the longing of days, and the lack I have
    won of the earth,
And the wrong amended by wrong, and the bitter wrong of
    my birth!'
She hath spread out her arms as she spake it, and away from
    the earth she leapt,
And cut off her tide of returning; for the sea-waves over her
    swept,
And their will is her will henceforward; and who knoweth
    the deeps of the sea,
And the wealth of the bed of Gudrun, and the days that yet
    shall be?

The whole poem then ends with a recapitulation:

Ye have heard of Sigurd aforetime, how the foes of God he
    slew;
How forth from the darksome desert the Gold of the Waters
    he drew;
How he awakened Love on the Mountain, and wakened
    Brynhild the Bright,
And dwelt upon Earth for a season, and shone in all men's
    sight.
Ye have heard of the Cloudy People, and the dimming of the
    day,

And the latter world's confusion, and Sigurd gone away;
Now ye know of the Need of the Niblungs and the end of
    broken troth,
All the death of Kings and of kindreds and the Sorrow of
    Odin the Goth.

Although the rhythms lack flexibility, they are energetic and powerful, and sustain the narrative thrust. Certainly Morris succeeds in his ambition of giving the English reader some idea of the Great Story of the North. There is also evidence on occasion of what may be seen as political implications, for example in the description of Sigurd's rule in Book Three :

Now sheathed is the sword of Sigurd; for, as wax withstands
    the flame,
So the Kings of the land withstood him and the Glory of his
    fame.
And before the grass is growing, or the kine have fared from
    the stall,
The song of the fair-speech-masters goes up in the Niblung hall,
And they sing of the golden Sigurd and the face without a foe,
And the lowly man exalted and the mighty brought alow :
And they say, when the sun of summer shall come back to
    the land,
It shall shine on the fields of the tiller that fears no heavy
    hand;
That the sheaf shall be for the plougher, and the loaf for him
    that sowed,
Through every furrowed acre where the son of Sigurd rode.

Sigurd is here shown behaving with the awareness of social responsibility of which Morris himself was becoming increasingly conscious.

Sigurd the Volsung has rhetorical qualities which make it read aloud effectively. It is ironical, therefore, that in Morris's day the idea of the public reading of poetry was simply never considered. For private reading, it suffers from the problem of all long poems, for the modern reader is used to a much more intense manner. The diffuseness which made *Sigurd* some four times as long as the original Icelandic narrative is its main weakness. But even the critic who made this point most wittily paid tribute to the overall success of the poem; Henry Morley's review in *The Nineteenth Century* in November 1877 remarked that, 'there is in almost every man a gift, which his fellows wish him to use sparingly, of saying in ten thousand words what he could say in ten'.[7] He went on to provide a poem of forty lines entitled 'The Lost Rune', in which an admirer of Morris was imagined lamenting the loss of his notebook. It concludes :

> So I yield to the will that is strongest, I marvel, and say, let
>   it be;
> It may lie in the glitter of Gimli, the bright elf-home of the free,
> Or be lost in the fireheat of Muspil, or buried in vapour and frost,
> Where Niflheim breeds the frost giants. This only I know, it
>   is lost.
> It is gone with the dews of the morning, it is gone with the
>   dreams of the day,
> For I make little notes upon paper and somebody takes them
>   away.

But Morley also noted that 'they only who have Mr Morris's genius could spin the yarn in Mr Morris's way; for at his longest he is still a poet, and his images, drawn from the beauty of the outer world, bring the fine sense of it home for us as none but the work of a true poet can'.

Morris was disappointed with the reception of *Sigurd*. According to Mackail, he felt that neither the critics nor the public appreciated it. In fact the critics seem to have praised the work with fewer reservations than *The Earthly Paradise,* but it certainly never made the same impression on the reading public : there was no second English edition until 1887. Since Morris never thought of poetry primarily as self-expression, and in this case was particularly keen to spread his Nordic gospel, the disappointment must have been considerable, especially by contrast with the popularity of his previous poems. When he was to turn again to narrative in his later romances the medium which he chose was prose. Fortunately he was a man of extraordinarily varied resources.

For an all-round view of Morris at this time, it is important to realise that all these business and literary activities were not allowed to destroy his private life. If his relationship with Janey was never to be fully restored, his friendship with Edward Burne-Jones and with Georgie remained firm, and those with his young daughters developed. May gives a very pleasant picture of one aspect of family life in her Introduction to Volume XXII of the *Collected Works* when she discusses her father's reading habits :

> I think perhaps there were no happier hours of our home-evenings than when, the winter wind tearing among the elms outside, we were gathered together round the great fireplace, Father reading aloud one of the family classics. We were presented with nothing harassing or ostensibly improving; it was all pure enjoyment, but no sleepy-hollow of vague harmonies, be sure. Our minds had to be on the alert to meet our varied and motley throng of friends those happy evenings, to follow their fortunes in the Highlands of Scotland, in the London slums, or overseas in the golden East. It was all very human and catholic, and very stimulating . . . It may sound grotesque to say it, but after all these years, a casual mention of Mr Jorrocks' lecture on 'Unting calls up, in a sudden pang of memory, a picture of autumn evenings round the hearth of the Tapestry Room at Kelmscott – beautiful harmonious times . . .

Favourite readings for these occasions were Scott, Dickens, Lane's *Thousand and One Nights*, Borrow, Cobbett, parts of the Icelandic sagas, the hunting stories of R. S. Surtees, especially *Handley Cross*. Morris had a great capacity for simple, wholesome enjoyment; he shared the high Victorian evaluation of family life, but freed it from the formality and authoritarianism which marked more conventional homes.

Despite the achievements of these years, however, Morris was by no means completely fulfilled. The incompleteness of his marriage, the arguments over the reconstitution of the Firm, the feeling that his products ministered in the long run only to 'the swinish luxury of the rich', Janey's serious illness in the summer of 1876, the lack of popular response to *Sigurd the Volsung* – these are elements in the more sombre side of Morris's thinking

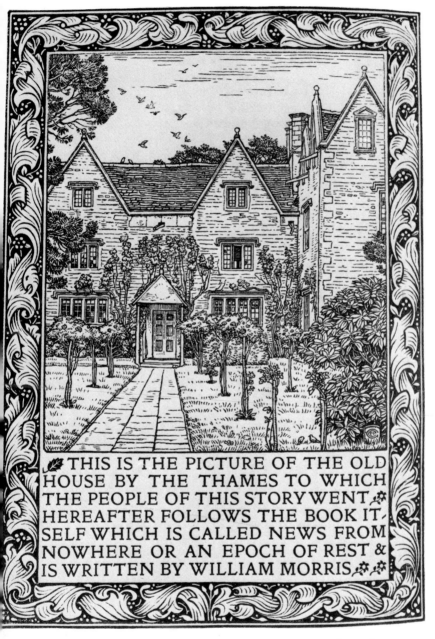

THIS IS THE PICTURE OF THE OLD
HOUSE BY THE THAMES TO WHICH
THE PEOPLE OF THIS STORY WENT
HEREAFTER FOLLOWS THE BOOK IT
SELF WHICH IS CALLED NEWS FROM
NOWHERE OR AN EPOCH OF REST &
IS WRITTEN BY WILLIAM MORRIS

Kelmscott Manor: frontispiece to News from Nowhere, *Kelmscott Press edition,*
1892. Victoria and Albert Museum, Crown Copyright

THE SUSSEX RUSH-SEATED CHAIRS
MORRIS AND COMPANY
449 OXFORD STREET, LONDON, W.

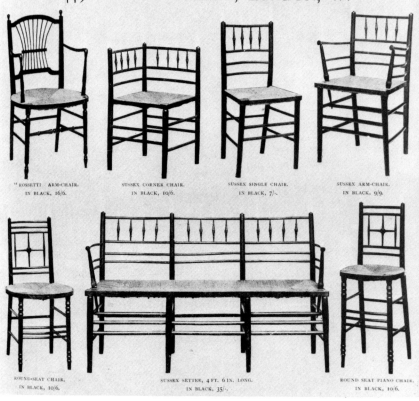

"ROSSETTI ARM-CHAIR.
IN BLACK, 16/6.

SUSSEX CORNER CHAIR.
IN BLACK, 10/6.

SUSSEX SINGLE CHAIR.
IN BLACK, 7/-.

SUSSEX ARM-CHAIR.
IN BLACK, 9/9.

ROUND-SEAT CHAIR.
IN BLACK, 10/6.

SUSSEX SETTEE, 4 FT. 6 IN. LONG.
IN BLACK, 35/-.

ROUND SEAT PIANO CHAIR.
IN BLACK, 10/6.

Advertisement for 'The Sussex Rush-Seated Chairs' from the Catalogue of Morris and Company, 1912. Victoria and Albert Museum, Crown Copyright

LOVE FULFILLED.

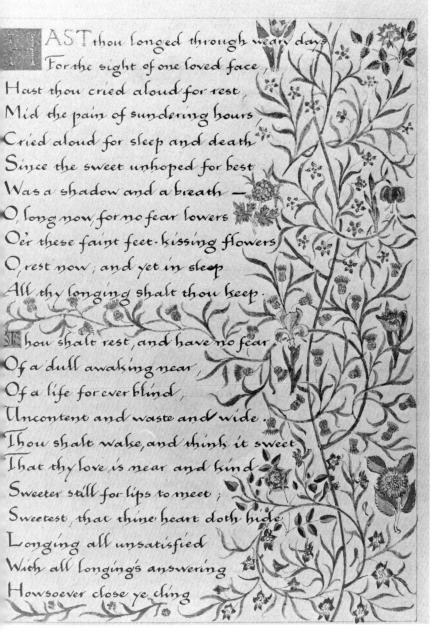

HAST thou longed through weary days
For the sight of one loved face,
Hast thou cried aloud for rest,
Mid the pain of sundering hours,
Cried aloud for sleep and death
Since the sweet unhoped for best
Was a shadow and a breath —
O, long now, for no fear lowers
O'er these faint feet-kissing flowers,
O, rest now; and yet in sleep
All thy longing shalt thou keep.

Thou shalt rest, and have no fear
Of a dull awaking near,
Of a life for ever blind,
Uncontent and waste and wide.
Thou shalt wake, and think it sweet
That thy love is near and kind.
Sweeter still for lips to meet;
Sweetest, that thine heart doth hide
Longing all unsatisfied
With all longing's answering
Howsoever close ye cling.

'Love Fulfilled' from A Book of Verse, *1870. Victoria and Albert Museum, Crown Copyright*

Woven wool: 'Bird', 1878. Victoria and Albert Museum, Crown Copyright

Stained glass: 'The Annunciation' from All Saints' Church, Middleton Cheney, Northamptonshire. Photograph by Sonia Halliday

Handknotted rug: Hammersmith Rug, 1888. Victoria and Albert Museum, Crown Copyright

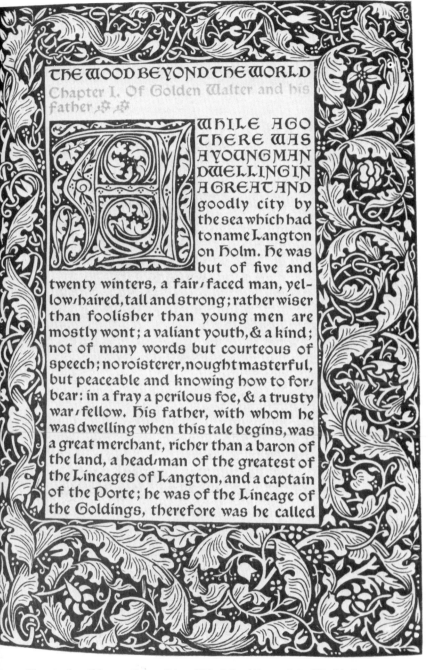

THE WOOD BEYOND THE WORLD
Chapter I. Of Golden Walter and his father

A WHILE AGO THERE WAS A YOUNG MAN DWELLING IN A GREAT AND goodly city by the sea which had to name Langton on Holm. He was but of five and twenty winters, a fair-faced man, yellow-haired, tall and strong; rather wiser than foolisher than young men are mostly wont; a valiant youth, & a kind; not of many words but courteous of speech; no roisterer, nought masterful, but peaceable and knowing how to forbear: in a fray a perilous foe, & a trusty war-fellow. His father, with whom he was dwelling when this tale begins, was a great merchant, richer than a baron of the land, a head-man of the greatest of the Lineages of Langton, and a captain of the Porte; he was of the Lineage of the Goldings, therefore was he called

Typography: Kelmscott Press edition of The Wood Beyond the World, *first page, 1894. Victoria and Albert Museum, Crown Copyright*

Wallpaper: 'Bachelor's Button', 1892. Victoria and Albert Museum, Crown Copyright

at the time, which occasionally finds expression in his letters. His reflections on reaching the age of 40 in March 1874 strike this note about London life :

> Surely if people lived five hundred years instead of threescore and ten they would find some better way of living than in such a sordid loathsome place, but now it seems to be nobody's business to try to better things – isn't mine, you see, in spite of all my grumbling – but look, suppose people lived in little communities among gardens and green fields, so that you could be in the country in five minutes' walk, and had few wants, almost no furniture for instance, and no servants, and studied the (difficult) arts of enjoying life, and finding out what they really wanted : then I think one might hope civilisation had really begun.

In the absence of this, perhaps the country needs 'some great and tragical circumstance' to provide it with 'a history and something to think about'. This 'sad grumbling', Morris ironically admits, may have been partly provoked by a wedding invitation which he lacks the courage to refuse although he feels such occasions are a waste of time. But clearly the feeling runs a great deal deeper : the ideas expressed remind us of Ruskin's and D. H. Lawrence's attacks on the modern industrial and urbanised world. At present it is simply 'grumbling', but it suggests the operation in Morris of a social awareness which will force him to become involved in wider public issues. There is an aspiration to make the idyllic feeling for the English countryside the basis for positive action, which sets Morris in sharp contrast with those who believed that industrial development was in itself a human good.

The first issue which actually led Morris into political action was a response to the views of the massacre of some 12,000 Christians in Bulgaria by Turkish irregulars in May 1876. This led to widespread fears of a Russian invasion in defence of the 'Christian' cause and an upsurge of anti-Russian feeling. The founders of the Eastern Question Association, however, resisted this hysteria and emphasised the injustice of the Turkish regime. Morris was an early member of the Association, and became its treasurer. A letter of 15 November 1876 to Charles Faulkner shows the depth of his feelings and a strong element of common sense :

> As to the Russians, all I say is this : we *might* have acted so that they could have had no pretext for inter-fering with Turkey except in accordance with the unanimous wish of Europe : we *have* so acted as to drive them into separate interference whatever may come : and to go to war with them for this would be a piece of outrageous injustice. Furthermore if we came victorious out of such a war, what should we do with Turkey, if we didn't wish to be damned ? 'Take it ourselves,' says the bold man, 'and rule it as we rule India.' But the bold man don't live in England at present I think; and I know what the Tory trading stock-jobbing scoundrel that we call an Englishman today would do with it : he would shut his eyes hard over it, get his widows and orphans to lend it money, and sell it vast quantities of bad cotton . . .
>
> I do not feel very sanguine about it all, but since it is started and is the only thing that offers at present, and I do not wish to be anarchical, I must do the best I can with it.

The man who does not 'wish to be anarchical' must be prepared to join public bodies, however far from ideal. Morris was now prepared to act in this responsible way, no longer satisfied with the role of 'idle singer'. The strength of his language about the middle-class to which he belonged is striking; it no doubt derived from his reading of Cobbett and Ruskin, who had both vigorously denounced the modern English preoccupation with money-making, and from his own experience in business. Morris's hostility to the age was now taking overt political form.

4

Into Politics, 1877–82

But in spite of all the success I have had, I have not
failed to be conscious that the art I have been helping
to produce would fall with the death of a few of us who
really care about it, that a reform in art which is
founded on individualism must perish with the
individuals who have set it going. Both my historical
studies and my practical conflict with the philistinism
of modern society have *forced* on me the conviction
that art cannot have a real life and growth under the
present system of commercialism and profit-mongering.
I have tried to develop this view, which is in fact
Socialism seen through the eyes of an artist, in various
lectures, the first of which I delivered in 1878.

About the time when I was beginning to think so
strongly on these points that I felt I must express myself
publicly, came the crisis of the Eastern Question and
the agitation which ended in the overthrow of the
Disraeli government. I joined heartily in that agitation
on the Liberal side, because it seemed to me that
England risked drifting into a war which would have
committed her to the party of reaction: I also
thoroughly dreaded the outburst of Chauvinism which
swept over the country, and feared that once we were
amusing ourselves with an European war no one in
this country would listen to anything of social questions;

nor could I see in England at any time any party more
advanced than the Radicals, who were also it must be
remembered hallowed as it were by being in opposition
to the party which openly proclaimed themselves
reactionists; I was under small illusion as to the result
of a victory of the Liberals, except so far as it would
stem the torrent of Chauvinism, and check the feeling
of national hatred and prejudice for which I shall
always feel the most profound contempt. I therefore
took an active part in the anti-Turk agitation, was a
member of the committee of the Eastern Question
Association, and worked hard at it; I made the
acquaintance of some of the Trades Union leaders at
the time; but found that they were quite under the
influence of the Capitalist politicians, and that, the
General Election once gained, they would take no
forward step whatever. The action and want of action
of the new Liberal Parliament, especially the Coercion
Bill and the Stockjobber's Egyptian War, quite
destroyed any hope I might have had of any good being
done by alliance with the Radical party, however
advanced they might call themselves.

I joined a committee (of which Mr Herbert Burrows
was a Secretary) which tried to stir up some opposition
to the course the Liberal government and party were
taking in the early days of this parliament; but it
speedily fell to pieces, having in fact no sort of practical
principles to hold it together; I mention this to show
that I was on the look out for joining any body which
seemed likely to push forward matters.

In this passage Morris describes this period of his life largely
in terms of his political development. While this was vitally
important to him, it did not mean a sudden change in his way of
life or an abandonment of his existing commitments, especially
to the Firm. It was a period of some uncertainty, as Morris
looked around for answers to the increasingly urgent problems
of the time while continuing many of his usual activities.

An unpretentious account of how Morris appeared at the
time is to be found in the series of 'Contemporary Portraits' in

The Dublin University Magazine in November 1878 entitled 'William Morris, MA'.[1] The article begins by suggesting that many people think of the author of *The Earthly Paradise* as someone quite distinct from the man of the same name who is 'head of a representative firm whose speciality has been the introduction of real art work into the common things of decoration and furniture', and then goes on to give a straightforward account of Morris's life and work. The achievements of the Firm are put into the context of Victorian values:

> It was so ideal a little guild that one marvels it did not fade away in a year or two like the Brook Farm community or a scheme of Pantisocracy. But work and will, patience and perseverance, so long as they are downright, and not merely sentimental, are as efficacious in producing solid results when wielded by young Oxonians and exquisite-handed painters, as when they are manifested by a group of navvies.

The Firm succeeded, that is to say, because the participants were prepared to work at the realisation of their ideals. But if Morris and his fellows shared the Victorian commitment to work – and Morris was to make important distinctions later on between 'useful work' and 'useless toil' – it was in the service of new ideals of beauty which the *Magazine* recognised as having greatly improved public taste: 'it is certain that the ideas of blue and green, of composition and design, to be seen now in the better class of shop are immeasurably superior to those of five-and-twenty years ago'. The Firm is praised for the high quality of its products, and for its organisation without the middleman and his exclusive concern for profit. Morris's poetry is then favourably discussed, and his liberal politics are remarked on: 'He takes a real interest in the course of events, though it would surely strain even his magical powers to show a poetical side to the average political life of the present day, notwithstanding the imaginative effects produced in its extreme attitudes.' This is rather obscure and contains elements of an easy irony about politics which Morris was no longer able to allow himself.

Morris continued his work for the Eastern Question Association in 1877. In May, after the Russian attack on Turkey

had brought feelings to greater intensity, he addressed a manifesto 'To the Working men of England' warning against war
in powerful language :

> Who are they that are leading us into war? Greedy
> gamblers on the Stock Exchange, idle officers of the
> army and navy (poor fellows!), worn-out mockers of
> the clubs, desperate purveyors of exciting war-news
> for the comfortable breakfast-tables of those who have
> nothing to lose by war; and lastly, in the place of
> honour, the Tory Rump, that we fools, weary of peace,
> reason and justice, chose at the last election to represent
> us. Shame and double shame, if we march under such
> leadership as this in an unjust war against a people
> who are not our enemies, against Europe, against
> freedom, against nature, against the hope of the
> world.[2]

Apart from the vigour of this attack on Disraeli and his government, the manifesto is notable for being directed to the working
class, who at this time of limited electoral rights did not possess
the vote. Morris nevertheless addresses them as 'fellow-citizens',
warning them that 'these men' – the nation's leaders – are as
hostile to their aspiration for a better life as they are favourable
to an unjust and unnecessary war. Morris was more impressed by
the MP for Morpeth, Burt, and other working-class leaders than
the confused responses of the Liberal Party to the crisis. A
popular music-hall song was preparing the English people for
war in the memorable jingle :

> We don't want to fight, but by jingo if we do,
> We've got the ships, we've got the men, we've got the money
> too!

The word jingoism, meaning war-like patriotism, derived from
this song, which was typical of the feelings which Morris and the
Association strove to control. When war seemed imminent in
January 1878 Morris wrote a ballad, 'Wake, London lads!'
which was enthusiastically sung at a meeting in Exeter Hall,
and marks a significant point in his development from his earlier

romanticism. Fortunately the danger of war receded with the Congress of Berlin in June, but by then Morris had become a much more political person. Despite his doubts about the Liberal Party, he worked for its success in the general election of 1880 which put an end to Disraeli's second ministry. He became treasurer in 1879 of the National Liberal League, an organisation formed from representatives of the more radical elements of the former Eastern Question Association, which attempted to keep the new government mindful of its election commitments. When it became obvious that the League was going to be ignored, Morris was glad to help wind up the organisation. Henceforward he was to seek political change through groups farther to the political left than the Liberal Party, which seemed to him half-hearted and ineffectual, especially in its Irish and imperial policies.

Morris had also become involved in another public body, more obviously related to his long-established interest in architecture and design. This was the Society for the Protection of Ancient Buildings, an organisation active and valuable in our own day which came into existence on Morris's initiative. Given his reverence for mediaeval architecture, it is not surprising that Morris was hostile to the Victorian fashion for the wholesale 'restoration' of ancient buildings. This often went much farther than the term might seem to imply; for instance, St Albans Cathedral is now almost as much the work of its wealthy restorer, Lord Grimthorpe, as of its original builders, and all four New Red Sandstone cathedrals – Worcester, Lichfield, Chester and Carlisle – show the results of vigorous restoration all too clearly, as do many less remarkable buildings all over England.

Restoration was often necessary in the nineteenth century; many of the buildings were in need of repair. It was the heavy-handedness of the operation in some cases that deserves criticism. The most prolific restorer of the Victorian period was the architect Sir Gilbert Scott, and it was his plans for Tewkesbury that led Morris to write an indignant letter to *The Athenaeum* in March 1877, choosing this paper because in it F. G. Stephens had been criticising Scott's restorations for a number of years. Morris's letter began pungently :

My eye just now caught the word 'restoration' in the

morning paper, and, on looking closer, I saw that this time it is nothing less than the Minster of Tewkesbury that is to be destroyed. Is it altogether too late to do something to save it, – it and whatever else of beautiful and historical is still left us on the sites of the ancient buildings we were once so famous for? . . .

What I wish for, therefore, is that an association should be set on first to keep a watch on old monuments, to protest against all 'restoration' that means more than keeping out wind and weather, and, by all means, literary and other, to awaken a feeling that our ancient buildings are not mere ecclesiastical toys, but sacred monuments of the nation's growth and hope.[3]

The response was immediate and vigorous. Within a month a meeting took place and the Society was founded, with Morris as its first secretary. It soon became an effective pressure group for what would now be called conservation, and Morris was to devote much energy to furthering its cause by speeches and writing. Its most spectacular early campaign, in 1880, was against the proposal to demolish and rebuild the western end of St Mark's, Venice, and replace the mosaics. The Italian government decided against these plans, though it is not clear to what extent such protests as those of the SPAB contributed to that decision.

Various changes in connection with the Firm occurred in these years. In 1877 new showrooms were acquired at 449 Oxford Street, enabling a wider variety of goods to be displayed, and also freeing the Queen Square premises for an extension of the production side. A carpet loom had been installed there in 1875 or 1876, and a carpet-knotter brought down from Glasgow to instruct the girls, but the cramped premises prevented more than experimentation. A silk-loom was set up in 1877 by a brocade-weaver brought from Lyons, and Morris's thoughts turned to tapestry. When Morris moved house from Turnham Green to Hammersmith in 1878, in the new residence – whose name he rapidly changed from The Retreat to Kelmscott House, to remind him of his Oxfordshire house, and which is now a lively centre for Morris studies – he had the carpet-looms installed in the old coach-house, and a hand-loom for high-warp tapestry in his bedroom. From the coach-house came a number of hand-tufted carpets and rugs, known by the name of Hammersmith and showing Morris's recognition of the need for greater conventionality of design than was the case with his earlier chintzes and wallpapers; one is shown in illustration no. 6. His interest in weaving at this time led him to study the woven textiles in the South Kensington Museum (now the Victoria and Albert), consisting then mainly of late Gothic and early Renaissance silks and velvets, with formal and symmetrical patterning. The influence of these materials can be seen not only in Morris's designs for carpets, tapestries and woven wool (see the 'Bird', 1878, illustration no. 4), but even in his wallpapers and chintzes, which became markedly less free and naturalistic.[4] The 'Sunflower' and 'Acorn' designs of 1879 both exhibit symmetrical 'turn-over' patterns which give a static effect, although the colours are full of life. It is more difficult to recognise the natural forms on which the designs are based, although Morris never moved into purely abstract forms. These designs are less attractive today than those, both earlier and later, where less formal patterning is obvious. But some of these patterns, like the 'St James' (1881) and 'Christ Church' (1882), were appropriate in their formality for the rooms for which they were first designed.

By 1881 the continued development of the Firm had made it obvious that the Queen Square premises were inadequate, and Morris was able to buy a disused print-works (once a silk-weaving factory) on the banks of the Wandle called Merton Abbey. This was only 7 miles from Charing Cross – though a difficult journey from Hammersmith, so that Morris had a room fitted up in which he could stay overnight when necessary. The only remnants of the abbey were a mediaeval wall. What remained was the river, with good water for the dyeing processes in which Morris was by now so expert, 7 acres of pleasant grounds, and a number of workshops, mostly long two-storeyed wooden sheds. Now at last it was possible to bring together all the work of the Firm in satisfactory premises, leaving Queen Square without regret. A circular issued at the time from Oxford Street specified twelve types of work made there : '1. Painted glass windows. 2. Arras tapestry woven on the high-warp loom. 3. Carpets. 4. Embroidery. 5. Tiles. 6. Furniture. 7. General house decorations. 8. Printed cotton goods. 9. Paper hangings. 10. Figured woven stuffs. 11. Furniture velvets and cloths. 12. Upholstery.'[5] Many of these crafts could now be carried on more efficiently and on a larger scale. For instance, the carpet-looms at Hammersmith had been 12 feet across; those at Merton were 25 feet. The making of high-warp Arras tapestries became possible, and a great expansion of chintz production took place. These were believed by Mackail to be the products which carried Morris's influence most widely into society, though as he noted few used them, as Morris recommended, for wall-hangings : 'People dressed themselves in his wall-hangings, covered books with them, did this or that with them according to their fancy; but hang walls with them they would not.'[6]

Stained glass was still first on the list of the Firm's products, but Morris himself was less involved now with new designs, as a good many had by now been accumulated and could be used again. Moreover, Morris's hostility to restoration expressed through the SPAB led him to question his early readiness to supply glass for old churches. He issued a circular explaining that 'we are prepared as heretofore to give estimates for windows in churches and other buildings, except in the case of such as can be considered monuments of Ancient Art, the glazing of which we cannot conscientiously undertake, as our doing so would seem to sanction the disastrous practice of so-called Restoration'.[7] This was undoubtedly a logical and moral decision, though its effect was simply to cause commissions for such work to go to other firms, often producing less good glass. Morris & Company were now dependent on new churches, and those which lacked architectural distinction – which for Morris meant anything later than the mediaeval period, including St Peter's, Vere Street, and St Philip's, Birmingham (the cathedral). The work at Jesus College Chapel was brought to an abrupt end.

By this time Burne-Jones was the Firm's only designer of stained glass, and he was developing his designs in a more pictorial direction, tending to see a large window as a single composition rather than a series of separate sections. Of course all large stained-glass windows have to have an overall sense of control, but this is not necessarily achieved in a pictorial way; it can be done by control of colour and juxtapositioning. Burne-Jones's way now, however – as his success as a painter increased – was to use methods of composition more like those in his paintings. It also seems that the glass-painters began to be given more responsibility for the background details, especially in the tracery lights, while greener quarries tended to reduce the earlier luminosity of effect. Nevertheless, a number of fine windows were made. The St Catherine window at Christ Church, Oxford (1877–8), in the south choir aisle, shows an effective contrast between the main figures in white and the deep blue and mauve backgrounds, while the angel-musicians in the tracery are particularly attractive. (These were the last windows supplied by the Firm to the cathedral). The east window at St Mary's, Tadcaster, is notable for its fifteen major figures in three runs separated by very vivid golden rays, for the highly successful colouring of which Morris was probably responsible. And the east window at St James, Staveley (1881), is again remarkable for its colour; six angel lights, by Morris, surround the two central Burne-Jones lights, 'The Ascension' and 'Christ on the Cross', but the backgrounds of all except 'The Ascension' are of a strikingly deep blue, scattered with golden, silver and red stars. This unusual effect gives unity and vitality to the whole fine window. Whatever the limitations Morris imposed upon the Firm because of his convictions, and however much Burne-Jones's success was encouraging him to leave details of his work to others, the Firm was still at times producing glass of the highest quality.

As Morris continued his work for the Firm, and committed himself to more public and political activities, it was inevitable that there should be a reduction in some other area, and this proved to be poetry. The poet who had written so voluminously in the previous decade was to produce only one other long poem, the Socialist *Pilgrims of Hope* (1885–6), although he continued to write some shorter poems, both political – constituting the *Chants for Socialists* of 1885 – and in his earlier modes – as published in *Poems by the Way* in 1891. It was a striking change, but not a conscious choice. In October 1879 he was writing 'As to poetry, I don't know, and I don't know. The verse would come easy enough if I had only a subject which would fill my heart and mind : but to write verse for the sake of writing is a crime in a man of my years and experience.' Since *Sigurd* no subject had seemed to him worth treating in poetry, and a new sense of social responsibility made him disinclined to write in the old ways. Thus it came about that his literary energies at this stage transferred themselves into the writing of his lectures, and he soon showed himself to be at least as effective a writer in prose as he was recognised to be in poetry. Both the writing and the delivery of the lectures came hard to Morris, who was no natural orator. But the effort that went into the planning and writing of them led to work of high quality, in which we are aware of a serious mind grappling with important questions in an impressively unshowy way.

The earliest of Morris's lectures, originally entitled 'The Decorative Arts' but now known as 'The Lesser Arts', delivered in December 1877, shows these qualities and is a very impressive first performance.[8] Morris begins by defining his subject : 'That great body of art, by means of which men have at all times more or less striven to beautify the familiar matters of everyday life.' Decoration is said to have two purposes : to 'give people pleasure in the things they must perforce *use*' and 'to give people pleasure in the things they must perforce *make*'. In discussing the latter point he refers with respect to Ruskin's account of the Gothic in *Stones of Venice,* arguing that the drudgery of work will disappear if all workers are given the chance to employ their innate abilities, because they will find fulfilment in so doing. Nevertheless, the underlying mood of the lecture is sombre, because Morris is well aware how far this ideal is from the realities of the age, in which regard for art is sacrificed to industrial growth. Perhaps, indeed, a 'dead blank of the arts' is the immediate prospect. Speaking of his own experience of the Firm, Morris repudiates advice that he must often have received :

> People say to me often enough : If you want to make your art succeed and flourish, you must make it the fashion : a phrase which I confess annoys me; for they mean by it that I should spend one day over my work to two days in trying to convince rich, and supposed influential people, that they care very much for what they do not care in the least . . . Well, such advisers are right if they are content with the thing lasting but a little while; say till you can make a little money – if they don't get pinched by the door shutting too quickly: otherwise they are wrong : the people they are thinking

of have too many strings to their bow, and can turn
their backs too easily on a thing that fails, for it to be
safe work trusting to their whims . . .

An irony is that Morris designs *did* become a fashion with the
aesthetes of the 1880s, but the more important point is Morris's
desire for a stable continuity of relationship to the public. Why
should good design be a matter of fluctuating taste? In fact
this takes us into a difficult area if we believe in free consumer
choice and the idea of change and development in design as in
everything else. The modern Western answer is to use advertising
as a means of controlling consumer demand, but Morris's words
show that he would have distrusted this – the Firm's advertising
was informative rather than persuasive – and it is true that
advertising encourages fickleness of taste, as evidenced in the
teenage market today. We may well sympathise with Morris's
desire for stability in this area, but it is not easy to see how
it can be achieved without reducing choice. This should serve as
a reminder that these lectures are not to be seen as high-flown
'literature', but as an honest attempt to grapple with problems
many of which remain unsolved today.

Equally problematic is Morris's next suggestion, that 'the
only real help for the decorative arts must come from those
who work in them': 'the handicraftsman, left behind by the
artist when the arts sundered, must come up with him, work
side by side with him'. Morris admits that there are 'stupendous'
social and economic difficulties in the way of this change, as
indeed there were and are. What he says makes sense in relation
to the crafts and perhaps small-scale industries like his own, but
it has little reference to large-scale industry which was coming
more and more to dominate the country. Morris can do little
more than offer a stroke of rhetoric against those responsible for
the new situation – 'those who are ridiculously called manufacturers, i.e. handicraftsmen, though the most part of them
never did a stroke of hand-work in their lives, and are nothing
better than capitalists and salesmen'. Morris then goes on to give
advice to those wishing to achieve his ideals, advising them to
study 'Nature and History', his own great inspirations. He then
effectively notes how inappropriate this advice must seem in
the squalid London of his time: 'how can I ask working-men

passing up and down these hideous streets day by day to care about beauty?' (Dickens's descriptions of London in such novels as *Bleak House* and *Our Mutual Friend* suggest vividly what Morris was referring to.) At least London is rich in museums, Morris notes – though they are closed on Sundays, the one day when working people could make use of them. However, if one can get outside London and into the country, there is still so much to enjoy. Morris is particularly eloquent here in writing about an England for which his affection becomes plain. This is the emotional centre of the whole lecture :

> . . . when we can get beyond that smoky world, there, out in the country we may still see the works of our fathers yet alive amidst the very nature they were wrought into, and of which they are so completely a part; for there indeed if anywhere, in the English country, in the days when people cared about such things, was there a full sympathy between the works of man and the land they were made for : – the land is a little land; too much shut up within the narrow seas, as it seems, to have much space for swelling into hugeness; there are no great wastes overwhelming in their dreariness, no great solitudes of forests, no terrible untrodden mountain-walls; all is measured, mingled, varied, gliding easily one thing into another : little rivers, little plains, swelling, speedily-changing uplands, all beset with handsome orderly trees; little hills, little mountains, netted over with the walls of sheep-walks : all is little; yet not foolish and blank, but serious rather, and abundant of meaning for such as choose to seek it : it is neither prison nor palace, but a decent home.

Morris's prose here is simple yet expressive, moving through the series of observations to the final clinching remark with its measured claim for what England can offer. He goes on to link 'this unromantic, uneventful-looking land' with the art that it gave birth to :

For as was the land, such was the art of it while folk
yet troubled themselves about such things; it strove
little to impress people either by pomp or ingenuity:
not unseldom it fell into commonplace, rarely it rose
into majesty; yet was it never oppressive, never a slave's
nightmare nor an insolent boast : and at its best it had
an inventiveness, an individuality that grander styles
have never overpassed : its best too, and that was in its
very heart, was given as freely to the yeoman's house,
and the humble village church, as to the lord's palace
or the mighty cathedral: never coarse, though often
rude enough, sweet, natural, and unaffected, an art of
peasants rather than of merchant-princes or courtiers,
it must be a hard heart, I think, that does not love it :
whether a man has been born among it like ourselves,
or has come wonderingly on its simplicity from all the
grandeur over-seas. A peasant art, I say, and it clung
fast to the life of the people, and still lived among the
cottagers and yeomen in many parts of the country
while the big houses were being built 'French and fine':
still lived also in many a quaint pattern of loom and
printing-block, and embroiderer's needle, while over-
seas stupid pomp had extinguished all nature and
freedom, and art was become, in France especially, the
mere expression of that successful and exultant
rascality, which in the flesh no long time afterwards
went down into the pit for ever.

Morris shows a superb command of language in this celebration
of the homely virtues of the English past.

Morris then gives some more practical advice on the education
of the craftsman, which should include drawing, especially of
the human figure, 'both because the lines of a man's body are
much more subtle than anything else, and because you can
more surely be found out and set right if you go wrong'. Finally,
Morris considers the social pressures of the time injurious to
the kind of art he believes in, the prevalence of 'sham'. This is
attributed to no single class, but to all classes, handicraftsmen,
the public, manufacturers; it is, however, the handicraftsmen
who are said to possess the remedy : 'The duty and honour of

educating the public lies with them, and they have in them the seeds of order and organisation which make that duty easier.' Morris again, perhaps thinking of his responsibilities so finely accepted in the Firm, seems unrealistic here, attributing an influence to his handicraftsmen which they no longer possessed in an industrial society. His later lectures show that he came to see this and its complement, the need for a more searching kind of class analysis. In 1877, however, he was writing in largely moral terms – like Carlyle and Ruskin – calling for an end to greed – 'wanting to be paid for what we have not earned' – and its divisive consequences. His strong feelings lead him to what those who think of him primarily as a decorator might find surprising conclusions: most of the decorative art of the time is not art at all, because it lacks the utility of true art; London houses are 'decorated' with 'tons and tons of unutterable rubbish – pretending to be works of art in some degree'. The true ideal is simplicity – 'Simplicity of life, begetting simplicity of taste'. The moral criticism is powerful as Morris reflects on his generation's lack of concern over the environment:

> Is money to be gathered? cut down the pleasant trees among the houses, pull down the ancient and venerable buildings for the money that a few square yards of London dirt will fetch; blacken rivers, hide the sun and poison the air with smoke and worse, and it is nobody's business to see it or mend it: that is all that modern commerce, the counting-house forgetful of the workshop, will do for us herein.

Morris goes on to suggest ways in which science, so highly regarded at the time but so often applied for merely commercial purposes, might help by 'teaching Manchester how to consume its own smoke, or Leeds how to get rid of its superfluous black dye without turning it into the river'. Concern for the human environment is central to Morris, and makes lectures like this still relevant today. The ending is an expression of faith in the ideal of a just human society which runs in and out of all Morris's writings. Though it is, he recognises, a dream, 'it lies at the bottom of all my work in the Decorative Arts, nor will it ever be out of my thoughts'. It was his courageous commitment to the dream which made Morris an inspiring influence to many of his contemporaries.

The Victorians, as traditional beliefs declined in their rapidly changing world, looked to their writers for guidance. Novelists like Dickens and George Eliot made direct social and moral comments in their works, while other prose writers gave their criticisms and advice in non-fictional forms. Writers like Carlyle, Ruskin, Mill and Arnold constituted the new literary phenomenon of intellectuals surveying the age with unparalleled freedom and breadth of view. Their ideas of what was wrong with society and what should be done about it were conveyed to the reading public through the important magazines of the time like *The Cornhill* or *Macmillan's Magazine* or *The Fortnightly Review*. Morris, with a wider public in mind, seldom published his lectures in these magazines, but he was practising an art that was already well established. His work, however, is markedly different in style from that of any of his predecessors. Carlyle often relies on a powerful and individual rhetoric, Ruskin on a biblical-flavoured eloquence, Arnold on a stylish urbanity and wit. By contrast Morris's lectures read very straightforwardly. Although, like any human argument, they possess structure and are organised, the structure is usually of a simple kind, and the argument enforced by a direct use of language with a limited range of reference and vocabulary. Morris's diction, especially since his immersion in the sagas, is largely Teutonic without either the nuances or the abstractions which the Latin element in English makes possible. He usually follows the rules about direct expression which George Orwell was to emphasise in 'Politics and the English language' as the basis of truthful political speech,[9] so that his lectures are more immediately readable today than much Victorian prose. In employing as direct and unrhetorical a style as he could, Morris was aiming to make himself intelligible to ordinary listeners and readers, an aim which again sets him to some extent against the age. The other writers favoured the idea of a wide readership, but only Morris worked at a prose style which might gain it.

In view of what has been said, it is unnecessary to analyse all his lectures; consideration of them here is chiefly concerned with them as evidence of the development of his ideas. 'The Lesser Arts' was followed by 'The Art of the People', delivered in

February 1879 in the Town Hall, Birmingham, as the annual presidential address to the Birmingham Society of Arts – a fact which again shows how Morris was moving more into public life. Many of the ideas echo those of the earlier lecture, particularly the stress on the intimate relation between art and society. Morris feels it less important to give advice on the practice of art than to argue that 'Art is a very serious thing, and cannot by any means be dissociated from the weighty matters that occupy the thoughts of men'. Morris believes that contemporary civilisation is indifferent or hostile to art, and that this means an impoverishment of the lives of millions of people. The point is made strikingly in a reference to the past : 'History (so called) has remembered the kings and warriors, because they destroyed; Art has remembered the people, because they created.' But that power of creation is now denied to the people by industrialism : that is the central problem, as Morris sees it. For even if some great political or social change occurred, man would still have to return to his 'daily labour'. Morris rejects one solution, that of shortening the hours of work and increasing the hours of leisure, with the question 'what shall we do with the leisure, if we say that all toil is irksome?' Here again he touches on an issue which is more important today than it was when he wrote. Is leisure what people really want? Can there be happiness without achievement? Morris believes that people must use their creative abilities in what he calls work – making things which are useful. He points out an ironical result of the expansion of the British Empire, which is that just as designers look to the art of the East for inspiration, that art is actually being destroyed by the new order imposed from Britain : 'The often-praised perfection of these arts is the blossom of many ages of labour and change, but the conquered races are casting it aside as a thing of no value, so that they may conform themselves to the inferior art, or rather the lack of art, of their conquerors.' As so often in reading these lectures, the reader finds himself confronted by facts which only need naming to appal – though the solution to the problems is by no means obvious.

Morris deals severely with those who would see art as a specialised activity suitable only for a refined elite. This idea – that of Aestheticism – was gaining ground at the time. The Conclusion of Walter Pater's influential book *The Renaissance*

(1873), originally part of his 1868 review of Morris's poems, had encouraged its readers to devote themselves primarily to the enjoyment of art because they would be most likely to find in it the 'fruit of a quickened, multiplied consciousness', since 'art comes to you professing frankly to give nothing but the highest quality to your moments as they pass, and simply for those moments' sake'. Admirers of Pater like Oscar Wilde took his ideas flamboyantly farther away from any sense of social responsibility, while the witty American painter James McNeill Whistler emphasised the idea of the artist as a master, totally separate from and superior to the times in which he lived. These ideas aroused Morris's contempt: 'It would be a pity to waste many words on the prospect of such a school of art as this . . . Its fore-doomed end must be, that art at last will seem too delicate a thing for even the hands of the initiated to touch; and the initiated must at last sit still and do nothing – to the grief of no one.' Morris's belief is in the contrary ideal of an art which is 'a good thing which all can share', such as was produced by the weavers of the East or the builders of the English parish churches. Thus the great evil of the day is that so many men have to do work which they despise and in which they can find no fulfilment, a situation out of which 'ruin must come in the end'. The way out of the situation is said to be through art. But since art is an abstraction, the question is really about the organisation of society: does it have the will to change towards giving men the chance of satisfaction in their daily work? Morris believes that this change involves conscious moral choices, especially concerned with honesty and simplicity. ('I have never been in any rich man's house which would not have looked the better for having a bonfire made outside of it of nine-tenths of all that it held.') The lecture ends with a moving appeal to its audience to 'work like good fellows by some dim candle-light to set our workshops ready against tomorrow's daylight'. The position is the same as in Morris's earlier lecture, but the problem of work in industrial civilisation is more fully enunciated. That his answer seems less satisfactory than his statement of the problem is not surprising when we realise that no solution has yet been achieved. Higher wages and increased leisure are the only obvious compensations which may be offered by society to workers with stultifying jobs, but it is not obvious that these are enough to fulfil the reasonable hopes of the modern worker. Yet Morris's ideal of 'an art which is to be made by the people and for the people, is a happiness to the maker and the user' remains ironically remote from the conditions of modern society.

Morris's lecture now known as 'The Beauty of Life' was given on a similar occasion in Birmingham a year later. Morris admits that it will not be radically different from its predecessor, but this time he lays more emphasis on historical developments, particularly the influence of the Romantic movement, with its recognition first of 'the romance of external nature' (as expressed by Scott) and then of the achievements of Gothic architecture. He gives a careful assessment of the nineteenth century – 'the Century of Commerce' – balancing its positive achievements against its 'recklessness' and 'blindness', and asserts that the way forward is through education : 'What remedy can there be for the blunders of civilisation but further civilisation? . . . You cannot educate, you cannot civilise men, unless you can give them a share of art.' Morris becomes indignant over the currently popular term 'the residuum', used of the lowest social class, arguing for the democratic view that society should 'aim at getting rid of this misery and giving some share in the happiness and dignity of life to *all* the people that it has created'. The most serious social problem is again said to be that of the 'un-mitigated slavish toil' in which so many workers are engaged. However, this time Morris asserts some more positive steps that may be taken. These include the preservation of fine buildings, like St Mark's in Venice or, as a footnote adds, Magdalen Bridge in Oxford; the prevention of 'restoration'; concern for the environment, as exemplified in the strict enforcement of the recently passed Act against excessive smoke – Morris mentions the good example of Sir Titus Salt's factory at Saltaire, the creation of an enlightened employer; the same concern expressed on a small scale in the avoidance of litter, 'scrawling one's name on monuments, tearing down tree boughs, and the like'; dislike of the hideous posters now showing the growth of advertising ('we ought to . . . make up our minds never to buy any of the articles so advertised'); preservation of trees on building sites (for which 'the little colony' at Bedford Park in north London is praised in a footnote – the planning of the estate there being in fact the work of men with principles influenced by Morris); and finally, improving the quality of housing for all classes. This would involve the renunciation of the demand for luxury, according to the new golden rule : 'Have nothing in your houses that you do not know to be useful, or believe to be beautiful.' Simplicity of furnishings and simplicity of life – this Morris offers as a bracing alternative to his age's preoccupation with ostentation and 'comfort'. These recommendations may seem obvious today and an anticlimax after the higher flights of the dream : but it is obvious that progress is made – and some has clearly been made since Morris's time – by taking these minor steps rather than vaguely hoping for Utopia to bring itself about. Morris in fact ends by making a striking reference to the widespread desire of his contemporaries for a definite moral framework in which decisions could be clear-out and bold – the mood of Arnold's popular poem 'The Scholar Gipsy'. Morris sees that 'visibly dying for a cause' must have its romantic appeal by contrast with 'the tangles of today', but asserts with unusual wit that 'tis clear that few men can be so lucky as to die for a cause, without having first of all lived for it'. Belief in the Cause – a capital letter appears in the final paragraph – must sustain its adherents amid the confusion of the present. It may be felt that Morris resorts here to a quasi-religious tone which works against the common sense of what he is saying, but the lecture as a whole is an impressive attempt to bring his ideals into action in the real world.

It was these three lectures, together with 'Making the Best of It' and 'The Prospects of Architecture in Civilisation', originally given in 1880 and 1881 respectively, that Morris brought together to form *Hopes and Fears for Art,* published in 1882. It was not widely reviewed, but Edith Simcox in the *Fortnightly Review* praised the 'little volume' for its 'rare and admirable breadth of view and firmness of grasp'. She accepted the argument of 'The Lesser Arts' that responsibility for social change must rest with neither the manufacturer nor the labourer, but interpreted Morris's 'handicraftsman' as 'mechanic' : 'Let the manufacturer and the mechanic moralise each other . . . but it is the mechanic alone who can moralise his labourer. The upper hundred thousand must set the fashion – of decent living – to the millions below them.' Victorian progressives could accept this model of social progress, but Morris himself was by now moving towards an approach which laid more emphasis on economic factors and less on moral effort.

A fine example of Morris discussing the crafts about which he knew so much is 'Some Hints on Pattern-Designing', which he originally gave as a lecture at the Working Men's College in London in 1881. It is in the *Collected Works* XXII. The lecture is lucid and thorough, and enables the reader to see some of Morris's basic principles as a designer. He defines pattern as ornamentation used for the sake of beauty and richness, and relates it mainly to the furnishing of an imaginary room. He seems to have in mind the idea of the members of his audience decorating their own homes, and encourages them to design their own patterns for the purpose. But in fact his advice is more suitable for men engaged in the production of decorative work – for designers like himself, in fact. Morris begins with general principles, emphasising that decoration should be suggestive not imitative :

> Is it not better to be reminded, however simply, of the close vine-trellis that keeps out the sun by the Nile side; or of the wild-woods and their streams, with the dogs panting beside them; or of the swallows sweeping above the garden boughs towards the house-eaves where their nestlings are, while the sun breaks through the clouds on them; or of the many-flowered summer meadows of Picardy? Is not all this better than having to count day after day a few sham-real boughs and flowers, casting sham-real shadows on your walls, with little hint of anything beyond Covent Garden in them?

Today we readily agree with this hostility to the realism that produces 'sham-real' boughs and shadows on flat surfaces, but we may feel that the solution to the problem is pure abstraction of design. This was never Morris's view : he argued that decoration should 'remind you of something beyond itself, of something of which it is but a visible symbol'. The emphasis is on 'the conventionalising of nature', and it is always the beauty and vitality of nature which are assumed to lie behind the designer's work.

Morris details the types of recurring pattern which can be

applied to flat surfaces – stripes, chequers, squares, diapers – and draws attention to the new motif which entered with early Gothic art by which 'continuous growth of curved lines took the place of mere contiguity, or of the interlacement of straight lines'. We can see that this principle of 'continuous growth' was the basis of all his own work as a designer. Morris then considers various crafts, showing his urgent belief in the necessity for the designer to have a deep respect for the craft for which he is working. He discusses wallpapers, cotton-printing, woven materials, tapestry, carpets, embroidery and pottery-painting (the last a craft which Morris practised comparatively little once he had met William de Morgan, whose work he liked and recommended to clients). In each case he shows his awareness of how the materials used should affect the designs made, and all his advice is admirably succinct and sensible. Typically, too he is hostile to abstraction even in carpet-design, though aware of the superiority of Eastern work :

> Now, after all, I am bound to say that when these difficulties are conquered, I, as a Western man, and a picture-lover, must still insist on plenty of meaning in your patterns; I must have unmistakable suggestions of gardens and fields, and strange trees, boughs and tendrils, or I can't do with your pattern, but must take the first piece of nonsense-work a Kurdish shepherd has woven from tradition and memory . . .

Morris is eclectic, working to incorporate the rich colours of Eastern carpets into his own pictorial view of decoration. But the principles remain clear; above all, the necessity to avoid vagueness and to express a 'rational growth' which will give vitality and unity to the design. Morris's own work is the finest vindication of the principle of 'rational growth' which he expresses so clearly in this and other lectures.

In view of these preoccupations it is not surprising that references to Morris at this time lay emphasis on his work as designer. In 1882 Walter Hamilton published a small book called *The Aesthetic Movement in England* in which he defended the movement from contemporary ridicule by showing the achievements that had stemmed from the influence of Ruskin and Rossetti. The account of Morris is brief and lacks personal involvement, but is suggests how he was then seen :

> William Morris, born in 1834, is by profession a designer of art decorations, wall-papers, carpets and such-like ornamental household necessaries, in which kind of business the new styles inaugurated and encouraged by the Aesthetes have created quite a revolution. He has recently published a volume of lectures on the decorative arts, in which the influence of Ruskin's teaching is strongly shown. He insists on the necessity of good, sound, honest work, both in art and trade, before all flimsy meretricious show and finery; he also advocates the opening of our art collections and museums to the public every day in the week; and the more general training of the people in the rudiments of artistic work.[10]

This is accurate as far as it goes, though it reduces Morris to a few simple beliefs rather than the impressively broad understanding of society which he was working towards at the time. By contrast, Morris would surely have been surprised to see how he was being presented to the American public by Oscar Wilde, then lecturing in New York on 'The English Renaissance of Art' :

> William Morris, substituting for the simpler realism of the earlier days a more exquisite spirit of choice, a more faultless devotion to beauty, a more intense seeking for perfection : a master of all exquisite design and of all spiritual vision. It is of the School of Florence rather than of Venice that he is kinsman, feeling that the close imitation of Nature is a disturbing element in imaginative art . . .

It was a high-flown discourse that the 26-year-old Wilde offered his audience. Morris would have disagreed strongly with the view of Nature attributed to him, and would have surely wondered where Wilde found the 'spiritual vision'. Later, he was credited with 'beautiful working in clay and metal and wood', some of the crafts in which he showed least interest. The end of the lecture referred directly to him and his ideas :

> For what is decoration but the worker's expression of his joy in work? And not joy merely – that is a great thing yet not enough – but that opportunity of expressing his own individuality which, as it is the essence of all life, is the source of all art. 'I have tried', I remember William Morris saying to me once, 'I have tried to make each of my workers an artist, and when I say an artist I mean a man.'

It is a peculiar achievement of Wilde's style to endow even Morris with a measure of his own affectation, although the idea *is* one that Morris might have expressed. There is also a strong effect of name-dropping – the men were only slightly acquainted – while the emphasis on individuality is very much Wilde's own. Yet it should be remembered that it was this very concept of individuality which Wilde made the basis for his argument for socialism in his witty, yet often convincing essay 'The Soul of Man under Socialism' (1891). All this is evidence that Morris was becoming more widely influential as a social thinker, as well as designer, and leaving behind to some extent his earlier reputation as a poet. Nevertheless it was in 1882 that Andrew Lang published his article 'The Poetry of William Morris' in the *Contemporary Review,* which is most interesting for its assertion of how Lang and his friends at college 'knew *The Defence of Guenevere* almost by heart, before the name of Mr Morris was renowned, and before he had published *The Life and Death of Jason*'.[11] Morris had come a long way since those days, though Lang says nothing of his social ideas.

In spite of his many involvements, Morris continued to spend as much time as he could with his family at Kelmscott Manor – the house in Hammersmith never being anything but a convenience to him. Evidence of his exuberant ability to relax and enjoy himself is to be found in the accounts of the trips made by family and friends along the Thames from Hammersmith to Kelmscott in both 1880 and 1881. High spirits and good fellowship prevailed and the periods in the country were truly

restorative. But they had to be paid for by renewed awareness
of contrasts. In the autumn of 1880 he was writing:

> I can't pretend not to feel being out of this house and
> its surroundings as a great loss. I have more than ever
> at my heart the importance for people of living in
> beautiful places; I mean the sort of beauty which
> would be attainable by all, if people could but begin
> to long for it. I do most earnestly desire that something
> more startling could be done than mere constant
> private grumbling and occasional public speaking to
> lift the standard of revolt against the sordidness which
> people are so stupid as to think necessary.[12]

After the 1881 trip and visit Morris delivered an address at the
town hall in Burslem entitled 'Art and the Beauty of the Earth'
in which he contrasted the two worlds of his recent experience,
Oxfordshire with its beautiful village churches and barns – 'the
works of the Thames-side country bumpkins, as you would call
us' – and London with its squalor and 'ruffianism':

> As I hear the yells and shrieks and all the degradation
> cast on the glorious tongue of Shakespeare and Milton,
> as I see the brutal reckless faces and figures go past me,
> it rouses the recklessness and brutality in me also, and
> fierce wrath takes possession of me, till I remember, as
> I hope I mostly do, that it was my good luck only of
> being born respectable and rich, that has put me in
> this side of the window among delightful books and
> lovely works of art, and not on the other side, in the
> empty street, the drink-steeped liquor-shops, the foul
> and degraded lodgings.[13]

The whole of Morris's thinking at the time was directed to the
uniting of these two Englands. It was soon to lead him to declare
himself a socialist.

5

Socialism, 1883–90

It must be understood that I always intended to join anybody who distinctly called themselves Socialists, so when last year I was invited to join the Democratic Federation by Mr Hyndman, I accepted the invitation hoping that it would declare for Socialism, in spite of certain drawbacks that I expected to find in it; concerning which I find on the whole that there are fewer drawbacks than I expected.

I should have written above that I married in 1859 and have two daughters by that marriage very sympathetic with me as to my aims in life.

Later Victorian politics was dominated by the long duel between Gladstone and Disraeli, two great politicians of totally contrasting temperament and outlook. The serious Anglican Gladstone led the Liberal Party, with its uneasy combination of belief in *laissez-faire* economics and in social justice to be brought about by the operation of the individual conscience. The flamboyant Disraeli, whose novel *Sibyl* in 1845 had coined the phrase 'The Two Nations' for the divided state of England, aimed to create a new conservatism that would unite all under the monarchy and give the nation a sense of purpose in the empire. Despite their differences, however, they had a good deal in common when it came to social policy. Both were aware that the development of industry was creating great problems that governments had to tackle, and took decisive steps in social legislation. But both accepted the overall economic structure of the country as providing the framework within which they must work.

Indeed, no alternative view was being put forward with any cogency in mid-Victorian England. The Jacobins of the 1790s and the Chartists of the 1840s might have expressed more radical views, but that was in the past. As England expanded economically, most felt that it was a matter of taking the new opportunities, and trying to mitigate by social reforms the sufferings engendered by the system. As power passed from the older ruling class to the rising bourgeoisie, so confidence in the future became stronger and it was possible to feel that the economic developments themselves would eventually solve the problems. But there were those who took a much less optimistic view. Writers like Carlyle and Ruskin implied that a totally new framework was necessary – though their tendency to locate the ideal in some kind of feudal order offended those enthusiastic about democracy. Marx and Engels too had formulated criticisms of capitalism which saw the way forward not in reform but in revolution, though their writings were not well known in England.

Morris had by this time come to the conclusion that the reformist approach did not go far enough; that the crisis of English industrial society could not be solved within the existing economic system. In a letter of June 1883, he wrote:

> Radicalism will never develop into anything more than Radicalism . . . It is made for and by the middle classes, and will always be under the control of rich capitalists: they will have no objection to its political development, if they think they can stop it there; but as to real social changes, they will not allow them . . .

His experiences with the National Liberal League had convinced him that neither of the existing political parties could fulfil his social ideals. But where was a new party to come from? By this time he had probably become aware of socialist groups on the continent putting forward anti-capitalist ideas, but, as E. P. Thompson has written, when he decided to become a socialist, Morris 'had almost no acquaintance with individual Socialists, no knowledge of the theory of Socialism'.[1] It was an act of faith, brought about by his profound dislike of the prevailing economic system which seemed to him to sacrifice all human ends to the amassing of profits. He then became truly a pioneer of English socialism, living through the perplexing early experiences of the movement. He was to commit himself consistently to the revolutionary side of the movement, in which the influence of Marx and Engels was deeply felt. He never had much sympathy with the reformist attitude of the Fabian Society, which attracted many of the intellectual elite of the era, including Bernard Shaw, H. G. Wells and Sidney and Beatrice Webb. He must have felt instinctively that the Fabians were Radicals at heart, rather than socialists. What he wanted was a social revolution that would alter the whole nature of industrial society. Seeking a group that would work with him to this end became the main political preoccupation of his later years. But whatever the problems of organisation and definition, he soon became a bold and resolute voice for socialism.

It was on 13 January 1883 that Morris joined the small Democratic Federation, having satisfied himself by attending its winter conferences on 'stepping-stones to Socialism' that it was by then a truly socialist organisation. The Federation was led to the Marxist approach by its leader, the ex-Tory H. M. Hyndman, who kept his top-hat after discarding the principles with which it was usually associated. A doctrinaire exponent of Marxism and a domineering personality, Hyndman was a genuine idealist, but it may be doubted whether his energy helped the cause of socialism in the long run.[2] However, at first Morris was prepared quietly to learn from those more experienced in politics and theory than himself, and he threw himself with enthusiasm into the work of the Federation, especially into public speaking, both as invited lecturer and on street-corners. The amount of work of this kind which he did in the next decade is staggering, as can be seen from Appendix I to E. D. LeMire's book *The Unpublished Lectures of William Morris*, 'A Calendar of William Morris's Platform Career'. This shows that in 1889 alone, for example, Morris attended sixty-three meetings, making speeches at most of them.

The lecture which marked his public commitment to socialism was 'Art under a Plutocracy', first delivered before the Russell

Club, a Liberal organisation, at Oxford on 14 November 1883. Morris begins with a discussion – which shows the continuity of his thought with the pre-socialist lectures – concerning 'what hindrances may be in the way towards making art what it should be, a help and solace to the daily life of all men'. The questions he puts to his audience are far-ranging:

> How does it fare therefore with our external surround-
> ings in these days? What kind of an account shall we
> be able to give those who come after us of our dealings
> with the earth, which our forefathers handed down to
> us still beautiful, in spite of all the thousands of years of
> strife and carelessness and selfishness?

Morris then divides art into two categories, intellectual and decorative, the former corresponding to the modern phrase 'fine art'. Although he recognises that some good work of this kind is being created at the time, Morris argues that the 'fine artists' are handicapped by having to work in isolation from their public. On the other hand, decorative art of any quality has ceased to exist, so that 'the words upholstery and upholsterer have come to have a kind of secondary meaning indicative of the profound contempt which all sensible men have for such twaddle'. Even worse is the fact that modern civilisation had destroyed so much of nature, to which man used to be able to turn for solace. Morris speaks eloquently against the appalling pollution that had taken place:

> To keep the air pure and the rivers clean, to take some
> pains to keep the meadows and tillage as pleasant as
> reasonable use will allow them to be; to allow peace-
> able citizens freedom to wander where they will, so they
> do no hurt to garden or cornfield; nay, even to leave
> here or there some piece of waste or mountain sacredly
> free from fence or tillage as a memory of man's ruder
> struggles with nature in his earlier days: is it too much
> to ask civilisation to be so far thoughtful of man's plea-
> sure and rest, to help so far as this her children to
> whom she has most often set such heavy task of grind-

ing labour? Surely not an unreasonable asking. But not
a whit of it shall we get under the present system of
society.

Morris goes on to deplore the urban, and suburban, squalor
which he sees spreading all over the face of a country which was
once beautiful. The writing is strong and urgent, the sense of loss
deeply felt. A final reference to the changes in Oxford itself over
thirty years should clinch for the audience the magnitude of
what is happening everywhere: 'the well of art is poisoned at
its spring'.

Morris then argues that this degradation is linked to the
economic system, with its reliance on the market mechanism of
uncontrolled competition, but suggests that this too will prove
only a phase of economic development. He gives a simple
Marxist explanation that sees the capitalist period of 'full-blown
laissez-faire competition' as bringing about its own crisis,
from which will emerge a new socialist order which
will 'substitute association for competition in all that relates
to the production and exchange of the means of life'.
Out of this new order will emerge a new, a renewed, art.
Morris summarises Ruskin's teachings as the belief that 'Art
is man's expression of his joy in labour', and looks forward to a
society in which that joy will be restored. He goes on to suggest
that the joy is compounded of four elements: the pleasures of
variety, of creative ambitions, of satisfying a social need, and of
exercising bodily skill. None of these pleasures is available to
the individual worker, who is therefore reduced below the status
of a slave to that of a machine. By contrast, the craftsman of the
Middle Ages, though often exposed to 'grievous material oppres-
ion', worked under conditions which made joy in his labour
possible. Morris elaborates the historical developments in some
detail, showing that some elements of this situation survived in
the workshops of the eighteenth century but were being extinguished in the nineteenth with increasingly large economic units:

> and when the process is complete, the skilled workman
> will no longer exist, and his place will be filled by
> machines directed by a few highly trained and very
> intelligent experts, and tended by a multitude of men,

women and children, of whom neither skill nor intelligence is required.

This system, it is suggested, is spreading unhappiness throughout English society.

Morris then seeks the cause of this social disaster. It is not to be attributed to 'machine-labour', or industrialism alone, for much labour is merely painful and needs to be eliminated or alleviated by the use of machinery. But the universal belief in the necessity to make a profit has meant that machinery is used only to increase production, not to lessen labour. It is not the 'machines and railways and the like' that are to blame, but the economic system that places profit before human values. Morris acknowledges that many are discontented with the system, but what most of those who desire change look forward to is a continuation of the class-divided situation, though with greater prosperity for the industrious worker – 'all the world turned bourgeois'. But to believe in the likelihood of this is to ignore the evidence of the last fifty years and the presence of a 'Class of Victims' unable to reach any kind of economic security, an inevitable part of the 'continuous implacable war' that is the essence of capitalist society.

The result of this system is waste, however orderly it may look because of its external discipline; Morris uses an extended military comparison to suggest this. The question which then arises is how the system can be destroyed when it is so strong : the answer lies in its internal contradiction, the fact that increasing economic scale creates larger and larger gatherings of workers, who will eventually be able to challenge the existing order. Those who think this unlikely to happen in England are morally indefensible because their hope is founded on the degradation of others. Those of the middle class who wish for a better future and a renewed art are urged to ally themselves with the 'reconstructive Socialism' represented by Morris and, by implication, the SDF. If the middle class can reconcile themselves to change, their attitude will help it to come about peacefully. To these Morris addresses a final appeal 'to renounce their class pretensions' – an emotively effective word – 'and cast in their lot with the working man', and not to be put off by any want of delicacy and refinement in the appeal. Perhaps they can bring that delicacy and refinement to the new movement by joining it. Morris's final argument is that 'organised brotherhood is that which must break the spell of anarchical Plutocracy'. Though a few men holding such a view may seem eccentric, with enough support the cause will achieve success. The responsibility is with those who see the situation as Morris does, and as he hopes his audience will.

The overtly socialist conclusion to the lecture aroused a good deal of controversy. The Master of University College protested, and a letter in *The Times* argued that Morris should have isolated art from political controversy. To have done so would have been to abandon the whole view of art which Morris had developed under the inspiration of Ruskin and which he found confirmed by his developing understanding of Marx. He read *Capital* in a French translation in February 1883 and found that its historical analysis supported and enlarged his own view. Morris's main contribution to the SDF was in subsidising the Federation's newspaper, *Justice,* which began publication in January 1884, and for which Morris wrote a good deal in that year. He was deeply concerned about the division of profits within the Firm – opponents pointed to the contradiction, or at least paradox, of his position as a socialist employer of labour. However, he decided, as a long letter to Georgiana Burne-Jones on 1 June 1884 shows, that he could make a better contribution to Socialism by 'the furthering of a great principle' (no doubt in such ways as the subsidising of propaganda) than by a division of profits, which would only result in £16 bonus a year when divided between the hundred workers of the Firm. Morris was a good employer; it is unlikely that he could have made as effective a contribution to socialism had he accepted the challenge he put to himself in the letter of trying to get his family to live on £4 a week. No man can avoid the historical limits of the time in which he lives, so that it is unfair to blame Morris for not having done so. He was certainly aware of the difficulties of the situation.

He was also becoming aware of tensions within the socialist movement. He became friendly with some of the younger socialists, like the Scot Bruce Glasier, who was to give an affectionate account of him later in *William Morris and the Early Days of the Socialist Movement* (1921), but also increasingly felt that Hyndman's leadership was turning the Federation into an autocracy. Together with the majority of the executive, including Belfort Bax and Edward Aveling, two of the most intelligent, Morris resigned. The next morning, 28 December 1884, he hired some rooms to act as headquarters for a new organisation, the Socialist League. Tactically it might have been better for Morris and his supporters – though he was a very unwilling leader and certainly never aimed to lead a new movement – to oust Hyndman. Members outside London would hardly be expected to understand what was going on, and tended to blame the Morris group. But Morris was no politician in the narrow sense, and it was no doubt with relief that he found himself in a position to continue his work for socialism without the overshadowing presence of his ex-leader.

Morris worked for the Socialist League with the same energy that he had shown for the Federation, but the split weakened both, and the strongly anti-parliamentary line taken by Morris tended to isolate the League and lead it towards anarchism – which Morris in fact disliked. Nevertheless, these years were productive. A new paper, *Commonweal,* was founded in February 1885, which Morris subsidised and edited. His main contributions included the socialist poem *The Pilgrims of Hope* in 1885 and the socialist romance *A Dream of John Ball* in 1886–7. *The Pilgrims* was to be Morris's last original long poem, and he was not finally satisfied with it, including only three sections of it in *Poems by the Way*. There is a certain awkwardness in the handling of the story, which concerns a pair of lovers whose relationship is broken by a male friend – the common triangle in his poetry – and death in the French Commune of 1870. Nevertheless, there is a good deal of insight into the situation of the unprotected wage-earner, both in relation to his employer and when unemployed. Of the passages retained by Morris, 'The Message of the March Wind' opens the poem and conveys the central message of forthcoming action. 'Mother and Son' is a dramatic speech addressed to a sleeping child in a direct manner derived from the Icelandic, remarkable in its sympathy for the woman's position in nineteenth-century society:

> Many a child of woman
> to-night is born in the town,
> The desert of folly and wrong;

and of what and whence are they grown?
Many and many an one
of wont and use is born;
For a husband is taken to bed
as a hat or a ribbon is worn.
Prudence begets her thousands;
'good is a housekeeper's life,
So I shall sell my body
that I may be matron and wife.'
'And I shall endure foul wedlock
and bear the children of need.'
Some are there born of hate,
many the children of greed.

When we remember the high evaluation of marriage and the home by the Victorians, and their shocked reaction to Hardy's ironical treatment of them in *Jude the Obscure* (1895), Morris is seen to be a bold and unorthodox thinker. The final extract, 'The Half of Life Gone', interestingly dramatises in soliloquy the internal conflict of a man whose sense of personal loss and sorrow threatens to stifle his desire for purposive action. We can feel in its regretful rhythms Morris's romantic self asking to be set free in a pastoral scene:

They are busy winning the hay,
and the life and the picture they make
If I were once as I was,
I should deem it made for my sake;
For here if one needs not work
is a place of happy rest.
While one's thought wends over the world
north, south, and east and west.

Morris was an energetic man, but that does not mean that he did not have to make a deliberate effort to act on many occasions. The nostalgia of 'If I were once as I was' suggests how much of an effort Morris was making in these demanding years of socialist activity. But the ending is characteristic too:

And thou, thou hast deeds to do,
and toil to meet thee soon;
Depart and ponder on these
through the sun-worn afternoon.

Morris was what the title of the poem implies, a pilgrim of hope.

His aspirations for humanity find finer expression, however, in the prose romance *A Dream of John Ball*. This, like many of Morris's favourite mediaeval works, is the first-person narrative of a man recollecting a dream; in this case, the dream had taken him back into the English past, of which two aspects had been particularly prominent: the 'garden-like neatness and trimness of everything', and the social situation in which his statement 'I am my own master' had provided the response 'Nay, that's not the custom of England'. It becomes clear that the dreamer is back at the time of the Peasants' Revolt of 1381, when John Ball had unsuccessfully led the peasants against their rulers, raising the subversive question, 'When Adam delved and Eve span / Who was then the gentleman?' In the final chapter, when the revolt has been defeated, the dreamer and John Ball, who is awaiting execution, discuss the future, and Morris is thus able to introduce the political issues concerning him deeply at the time. The language of the romance is simple and dignified, as in Ball's words of farewell: 'I wish thee what thou thyself wishest for thyself, and that is hopeful strife and blameless peace, which is to say in one word, life. Farewell, friend.' The book ends with the dreamer's awakening to the 'wretched-looking blue-slated houses' of nineteenth-century London, with its air of 'dirty discomfort', while the hooters call the workers to their factories. But the reader has been convinced that the ideal of fellowship, as preached by John Ball, however often defeated, is essential to humanity and perhaps may one day be realised on earth. The romance is thus both moving and inspiring, and suggests the depth of Morris's commitment to the socialist cause as he understood it.[3]

His commitment to socialism saddened some of his old friends – it was never really understood by Burne-Jones – and annoyed supporters of the status quo. Writers in *The Saturday Review* were particularly hostile. Their sophisticated, worldly-wise conservatism found Morris's idealism embarrassingly naive – a product of the 'Cloud-Cuckoo-Land at Hammersmith' to which it ironically referred (in Greek) in an article in January 1885: 'A Society for the Utter Abolition and Total Suppression of Discontent! Can it be possible that in any of the other seventy-four comedies *dont L'Eternal s'amuse* a more amusing scene has recently been put on than the solemn formulation of such a project?' But the *Review* also asked the most pertinent question which can be directed to a Marxist: 'One of his pithy remarks, according to the interviewer, was "Competition develops its opposite – Socialism". And would not Socialism develop its opposite – competition? All things are double, one against another is an uncommonly true saying, no doubt; but it is as true for one end of the pair as for the other.' Once the dialectical process of history has been accepted, the Marxist can only move out of it by the metaphysical decision to decree the end of history. Morris never confronted this problem, because his sense of crisis told him that immediate issues must be the present concern.

The Saturday Review had another chance to get at Morris when he was arrested and appeared in court on charges arising from an open-air meeting at the corner of Dod Street and Burdett Road in September 1885. He was discharged by the magistrate on the grounds of there being insufficient evidence of disorderly conduct and striking a policeman. The *Review* used the occasion to address some poetic advice to Morris as 'The Poet in the Police-Court', now unfortunately consorting with 'Germans and Cockneys, long of hair and ear', and calling on the Muses to reclaim him from politics:

> Were it not better that ye bore him hence,
>   Muses, to that fair land where once he dwelt,
>   And with those waters at whose brink he knelt
> (Ere faction's poison drugged the poet-sense)
>   Bathed the unhappy eyes too prone to melt
> And see, through tears, man's woes as man's offence?
>
> Take him from things he knoweth not the hang of,
>   Return his fancy and snuff out his 'views',
> And, in the real Paradise he sang of,
>   Bid him forget the shadow he pursues.[4]

Similar advice had been given to earlier writers like Ruskin and Dickens who had found that the state of Victorian society was so disturbing that they must make its reformation their central concern.

All these political activities were additional to Morris's continuing contributions at the Firm, though these necessarily decreased somewhat. Fortunately the move to Merton Abbey had made for greater efficiency, and George Wardle and F. and R. Smith could look after the day-to-day management. The amount of stained glass produced had decreased owing to Morris's decision not to supply it for work of restoration, but ambitious work was produced in these years, particularly for St Philip's Church (now the cathedral), Birmingham. The east window of the chancel, by Burne-Jones in 1885, is a large, rounded-headed window in the eighteenth-century baroque style in which the whole cathedral was built by Thomas Archer in 1715. It was installed when J. A. Chatwin had enlarged the apse to give greater prominence to the altar. Burne-Jones was pleased with the window, which represents the Ascension, with Christ in red set in a rather dark ensemble of blue and green, enlivened with white. Burne-Jones's comments in his account book for the Firm, in which he recorded both facts and often facetious comments, describe what happened next :

> It was in the year (I was about to say of Grace) 1885 that visiting my native city of Birmingham I was so struck with admiration of one of my works in St Philip's Church – (may I mention parenthetically that in that very church at the tender age of a few weeks I was enlisted in the rank and file of the church militant) struck with admiration at my own work (a naive confession which all others will condone) I undertook in a moment of enthusiasm to fill the windows on either side with compositions which I hoped and perhaps not unreasonably hoped to make worthy of my former achievement. In the glow of the moment, carried out of myself with a sort of rapture, and as it were defenceless against the shafts of the avaricious and the mercantile I made no pecuniary stipulation . . .[5]

Eventually he charged £200 each for the cartoons, a moderate price considering the scale of the windows and his popularity as an artist at the time. The two windows, finished in 1888, were a Nativity and a Crucifixion, and they employ the same range of colours. Together they contribute a powerful climax to the chancel, and a dramatic contrast with the lightness of the nave. A west window of the Last Judgement was installed in 1897.

Another large commission of those years was for the Chapel of St Ursula at Whitelands Training College, then in Chelsea. (The windows are now in the college's 1930 chapel in Putney.) The windows mostly represent female saints, and again employ Burne-Jones's favoured colours, especially blue and red, to sombre effect. The development of Burne-Jones towards a more pictorial style and an ethereal rendering of the figure can be seen in these windows, and perhaps more clearly in churches which contain both earlier and later glass. All Hallows, Allerton, Liverpool, is a good example, since it contains thirteen windows from 1875 through to 1887. The River of Paradise east window has already been discussed as showing a movement into pictorialism, but his tendency is even more marked in the later windows, the Nativity, Baptism and Christ Disputing with the Doctors. Now the figures are larger and more stylised, and the overall composition is less dynamic. There is none of the attractively Morrisian foliage and flowers which give life to the four-light windows in the transept, or the quiet dignity attained by the unusual white and brown colouring of the figures in the west window of 1876. An even more striking example of the development can be seen in St John the Evangelist, Torquay. The east window of 1865 contains ten small figures, all by Burne-Jones, in two tiers, with an attractive range of turrets by Philip Webb above the upper range. The colour is varied, and includes a good deal of white, and the effect is fresh and attractive. By contrast the larger west window of 1890, representing the Angelic Hierarchy, is far more dramatic. Colour is used expressively, one colour for each large figure, and there is a much greater sense of deliberation about the effects. What we now know as the Burne-Jones style is far more obvious here. Clearly Morris was leaving much more of the responsibility for such windows to his partner and the Firm's glass-painters, Bowman, Stokes and Dearle.

Between 1883 and 1890 Morris designed ten wallpapers and seven chintzes. The majority of these designs (which retain the formality of the previous period) exhibit a new structural emphasis on the diagonal. Peter Floud argued convincingly that Morris derived the new emphasis from a fifteenth-century Italian cut velvet acquired by the South Kensington Museum in 1883, the organisation of which he followed also in arranging the flowers on either side of the diagonal stem to constitute a subsidiary grid on vertical and horizontal axes, to give stability.⁶ The chintzes of this period take their names from English rivers, and include 'Evenlode' (used for the cover of the present volume), 'Kennet', 'Wandle', 'Lea' and 'Medway'. The diagonal axis helps to give movement to these designs, which are nevertheless firmly controlled, with largely conventional details. The effect in such a textile as 'Evenlode' is both rich and vital. In the later 1880s Morris's chief designer at Merton Abbey, J. H. Dearle, was himself producing a number of textile designs, and there may have been some co-operation. Experts find it difficult to differentiate these designs after 1885. The wallpapers either continue the 'turn-over' patterns of the previous period, as in 'Lily and Pomegranate' (1886) and 'Autumn Flowers' (1888), or employ the same diagonal structure as the chintzes, as in 'Wild Tulip' (1884), 'Bruges' (1888) and 'Norwich' (1889). They show the extraordinary fecundity of Morris's imagination even at a time when his political concerns were so intense and demanding.

The move to Merton Abbey had made possible the development of tapestry weaving on the high-warp loom, and Morris produced several successful designs including 'Woodpecker' and 'The Forest'. For these he wrote a number of brief and charming poems, published in *Poems by the Way* (1891). 'Pomona' is a particularly attractive example :

> I am the ancient Apple-Queen,
> As once I was so am I now.
> For evermore a hope unseen
> Betwixt the blossom and the bough.
>
> Ah, where's the river's hidden gold !
> And where the windy grave of Troy?
> Yet come I as I came of old
> From out the heart of Summer's joy.

Morris was always prepared to use poetry to enhance a suitable context, not giving it an isolated aesthetic status. For him it was simply part of the beauty of life, not a key to higher truths. Thus it could consort easily with his work as a designer.

The Merton Abbey works attracted some attention as the

reputation of the Firm developed and, later, as Morris's political involvement became better known. Two accounts of the 1880s give a very favourable impression of the works. An anonymous article in the *Spectator* in November 1883 entitled 'On the Wandle' was enthusiastic about both Morris's works and the neighbouring pottery of William de Morgan, who shared the same view of his craft :

> What is the real secret of the refreshing atmosphere which clings about these workshops of William Morris and William de Morgan? Wherein lies the immense difference in the influence on us produced by their work and the ordinary manufactured stuffs, stained glass, and pottery? . . . The genius of inventiveness and the love of beauty are the ruling principles, not the making of money.[7]

A more ecstatic note was struck by the American poet and essayist Emma Lazarus, in 'A Day in Surrey with William Morris' in the *Century Magazine* in July 1886. She enthused over the prettiness of the little village railway stations on her way to Merton, and over the works on her arrival. Nevertheless, she was thorough and observant :

> In the first outhouse that we entered stood great vats of liquid dye, into which some skeins of unbleached wool were dipped for our amusement; as they were brought dripping forth, they appeared of a sea-green color, but after a few minutes exposure to the air, they settled into a fast, dusky blue. Scrupulous neatness and order reigned everywhere in the establishment; pleasant smells as of dried herbs exhaled from clean vegetable dyes, blent with the wholesome odour of grass and flowers and sunny summer warmth that freely circulated through open doors and windows. Nowhere was one conscious of the depressing sense of confinement that usually pervades a factory; there was plenty of air and light even in the busiest room, filled with ceaseless din of whirring looms where the artisans sat bending over their threads; while the lovely play of colour and

beauty of texture of the fabrics issuing from under their fingers relieved their work of that character of purely mechanical drudgery which is one of the dreariest features of ordinary factory toil. Yet this was evidently the department that entailed the most arduous and sedentary labour, for as we went out again into the peaceful stillness of the July landscape, Mr Morris reverted with a sigh to the great problem, and asked why men should be imprisoned there for a lifetime in the midst of such deafening clatter, in order to earn a bare subsistence, while the average professional man pockets in comfortable ease a fee out of all proportion to his exertions?[8]

It was Morris's insistence on asking such questions which set him most markedly against his age, and which gave him the background for such lectures as 'Useful Work versus Useless Toil'.

In *Signs of Change* (1888) Morris brought together seven of his socialist lectures: 'How We Live and How We Might Live', 'Whigs, Democrats, and Socialists', 'Feudal England', 'The Hopes of Civilization', 'The Aims of Art', 'Useful Work versus Useless Toil' and 'Dawn of a New Epoch'. No doubt Morris felt that these had been the most effective of his recent lectures; they do not differ markedly in theme or quality from others of the period included by May Morris in the *Collected Works,* Vol. XXIII. Particularly successful is 'Useful Work versus Useless Toil', with its powerful attack on the common Victorian assumption, encouraged by the writings of Carlyle, that all work was desirable – a belief, as Morris points out, more usually held by the affluent:

In short, it has become an article of the creed of modern morality that all labour is good in itself – a convenient belief to those who live on the labour of others.

Under capitalism, Morris argues, the workers toil while the affluent are idle. In a socialist society, based on equality, 'All must work according to their ability, and to produce what they consume'. Each worker would reap the benefits of his work in material rewards and in leisure. He would also – and here Morris is conscious of going beyond the claims of other socialists for whom these two achievements would be enough – receive some 'compensation for the compulsion of nature's necessity' :

> As long as the work is repulsive it will still be a burden which must be taken up daily, and even so would mar our life, even though the hours of labour were short. What we want to do is to add to our wealth without diminishing our pleasure. Nature will not be finally conquered till our work becomes part of the pleasure of our lives.

Here Morris raises a fundamental question about industrial civilisation; for him, socialism is a system which will not only give greater equality of possessions, but will solve the problem of 'useless toil', work felt to be repulsive and dehumanising. To raise such questions shows Morris's foresight, since it is the twentieth century's inability so far to answer them that accounts for many of our current discontents. He was aware that his own suggested answers might seem 'strange and venturesome'; that they still do suggests how difficult the problems have proved. Morris's suggestions are that labour must be made socially useful, restricted in hours, varied – 'a man might easily learn and practise at least three crafts' – and in pleasant surroundings. Factories, where necessary for large-scale production, might offer 'opportunities for a full and eager social life surrounded by many pleasures'; apart from tending the machinery, the workers might work on the surrounding land and participate in 'the study and practice of art and science'. And the factories themselves would be made less cramped and dirty :

> Science duly applied would enable them to get rid of refuse, to minimise, if not wholly to destroy, all the inconveniences which at present attend the use of elaborate machinery, such as smoke, stench and noise; nor would they [the workers] endure that the buildings in which they worked or lived should be ugly blots on the fair face of the earth.

To the argument that such improvements would greatly raise prices, Morris replies in several ways : there would be more workers, with the elimination of a parasitic leisure class; neither luxuries nor cheap wares would any more be needed; and, more significantly, machinery could be put to the proper use of reducing labour rather than increasing profits :

> In a true society these miracles of ingenuity would be for the first time used for minimising the amount of time spent in unattractive labour, which by these means might be so reduced as to be a very light burden on each individual.

The sharing of work unattractive to all would be a socially acceptable way of getting it done. The emphasis on machines here is important. Morris's argument that they should be made in reality what they were often claimed to be – 'labour-saving' – is impressive, as indeed is the whole lecture. We have moved in some ways towards these ideals suggested in it, in that modern factory conditions are physically far better than those of the nineteenth century, but it can hardly be argued that the modern factory is the kind of social institution which Morris envisaged. It is an open question whether his ideal is extravagant or our achievement inadequate. What is clear is that, contrary to some widely held views, Morris did envisage science and machinery as playing a constructive part in the human future. It is unfortunate that he did not include the complementary essay 'A Factory as It Might Be' (published in *Justice* in 1884 but not apparently given as a lecture) in *Signs of Change;* May Morris also omitted it from the *Collected Works.* Its inclusion would have strengthened the reader's sense of the realism of Morris's attitude to contemporary society.

The political position of the Socialist League is demonstrated by two reviews of *Signs of Change* : *The Saturday Review* called it 'The Earthly Inferno' ('Under the system of competition, the evils which Mr Morris would abolish by Socialism, are gradually curing themselves'), while *Today,* the journal of the recently established reformist Fabian Society, feared that it would frighten off possible converts by its insistence on the class war : 'To sum up, socialists will do well to buy Mr Morris's latest book, for they will derive therefrom much pleasure and some profit, but they had better keep it to themselves and not lend it to their, as yet unconverted, acquaintances.' The issue which these reviews raise is still central to the debate about socialism in England. Is the reformist method of the Fabian Society capable of bringing about the changes which socialists desire? Others still contend that 'the evils . . . are gradually curing themselves'. Morris's view was that reform could not accomplish enough; more sweeping changes were necessary.

In literature Morris now turned to translating the *Odyssey,* a task undertaken as a partial relaxation from politics. He had an unusual ability to use his energies constructively; most men would have relaxed in a less creative way. Using the energetic verse-form of *Sigurd,* Morris produced a vigorous translation, published in 1887–8, which earned the approval of the classical scholar E. D. A. Morshead in *The Academy*: 'Of all verse translations of Homer that I have seen this seems to me to be the best, to have most of the matter and manner of the original.' Oscar Wilde, too, originally a classical scholar, praised the translation in the *Pall Mall Gazette* : 'Its fidelity to the original is far beyond that of any other verse-translation in our literature, and yet it is not the fidelity of the pedant to his text but rather the fine loyalty of poet to poet.' Both reviewers were aware that Morris had been criticised for his 'mannerisms' and the archaism of his diction, but rejected the criticism. Mowbray Morris, however, in the *Quarterly Review* in October 1888, severely criticised Morris's translation for the 'clumsy travesty of an archaic diction' which had 'overlaid Homer with all the grotesqueness, the conceits, the irrationality, of the Middle Ages'. And in the same magazine in July 1889, the classical scholar R. Y. Tyrrell, discussing translations of Virgil, criticised Morris's on the grounds of its unsuitable 'old-world tone' and 'the sense of incongruity inspired by such Wardour-Street English as *eyen* and *chepe*'.[9] (Wardour Street was noted for the production of sham antique furniture.) An important question about Morris's later prose fictions concerns his deliberate use of an archaic language unlike that which he used in his lectures. The question goes deep, and is related to the coexistence in Morris of a love of some aspects of history and an intense concern about the future of humanity.

The works produced during the period of Morris's early membership of the Socialist League, most of which originally appeared in *Commonweal,* are *The Pilgrims of Hope,* and *A Dream of John Ball.* Then came the calamitous experience in Trafalgar Square on 12 November 1887, when the large contingents of demonstrators were easily defeated and scattered by the disciplined aggression of the police. The experience of participating in this demonstration deeply affected both Morris and Shaw. The latter drew the conclusion that a successful revolution was inconceivable in England and turned to a thorough-going reformism. Morris was forced to see that his hope of sudden revolutionary change was false, but he continued to believe that revolution, however delayed, was the necessary pre-requisite for the establishment of Socialism. His later writings bear the marks of this enforced longer perspective without losing their revolutionary basis.

A Tale of the House of the Wolfings (1889) was the first of the less directly political romances which Morris was to produce in the last part of his life, but its emphasis on communal identity of the Gothic tribe with which it deals, in contrast to the individualism and commercialism of the Romans with whom they are in conflict, has clear political implications. The opening sentence will give some idea of the unusual stylistic qualities of these romances (and in *The Wolfings* there are also long passages of poetry):

Chapter 1   The Dwellings of Mid-Mark ·

The tale tells that in times long past there was a dwell-ing of men beside a great wood. Before it lay a plain, not very great, but which was, as it were, an isle in the sea of woodland, since even when you stood on the flat ground, you could see trees everywhere in the offing, though as for the hills, you could scarce say that there were any; only swellings-up of the earth here and there, like the upheavings of the water that one sees at whiles going on amidst the eddies of a swift but deep stream.

Language is being used in a way felt appropriate to the primitive Gothic peoples with whom the story deals; Morris avoids words of Latin origin, and uses a simple syntax, with semi-colons rather than subordinate clauses. The effect is of a primitive simplicity.

The story concerns the eventual defeat of the Romans by the Wolfings, and is focused on the figure of the Wolfings' leader Thiodolf (Folkwolf). Thiodolf, who is not a Wolfing by blood, keeps a mistress, the Wood-Sun (a Valkyrie expelled from God-home for giving herself to Thiodolf). She lives in the forest, and when she hears of the forthcoming warfare gives Thiodolf a magic hauberk to protect him. When he wears it, he is kept safe, but at the expense of the Wolfings. He comes to see that it is 'for the ransom of a man and the ruin of a folk'; he becomes alienated from his former friends. Only when he rejects the hauberk and the individualism that it represents can he become one with the Wolfings again. When the decision is made, he can address the Wood-Sun with renewed self-respect :

> 'Look at me, O Wood-Sun, look at me, O beloved ! tell me, am I not fair with the fairness of the warrior and the helper of the folk ? Is not my voice kind, do not my lips smile, and mine eyes shine ? See how steady is mine hand, the friend of the Folk ! For mine eyes are cleared again, and I can see the kindreds as they are, and their desire of life and scorn of death, and this is what they have made me myself.'

Thiodolf now leads the Wolfings to victory; although he is killed in the battle, his action has finally made him one with the folk. The story is a powerful reworking of some themes from the Icelandic literature which Morris loved, by a mind deeply hostile to the individualism of the age, but convinced of the need for human choice and commitment.

Morris had allowed his earlier books to be produced in the normal manner and forms of the publishers of the time, without much regard for typography and visual effect. Now, however, he began to interest himself in yet another craft, that of book production. He supervised *The Wolfings* through the Chiswick Press, and carried his innovations further in *The Roots of the Mountains* (1890). This is another romance dealing with a Germanic tribal community under threat, though this time from the Huns some centuries later. It is a much longer work, all in prose (as indeed are all the later romances), and suffers from its diffuseness. Morris was writing these romances largely for his own pleasure, and his habit had always been to elaborate rather than to dramatise; so the diffuseness is not surprising. It does not destroy the interest of the story, in which the men of Burgdale succeed in defeating the Dusky Men partly by their own determination and partly by being reunited with long-divided kinsmen. Two marriages at the end emphasise the new unity. The hero is Face-of-god, the Son of the Alderman or leader of the tribe, and the reader is kept close to his consciousness. Face-of-god leaves the Dale and the girl to whom he is betrothed, called the Bride, driven by an inexplicable youthful restlessness. He meets the Sunbeam, with whom he falls in love, and whose tribe joins with the men of Burgdale in defeating the encroaching Huns. From being 'one against the world' he becomes a responsible leader of his folk. It appears that a true scheme of values is to be reached by experience, not simply accepted from tradition. And it may involve suffering – perhaps in those who do not deserve it, in this case the Bride. It is notable that Morris endows the female characters in the romances with a directness and strength that is unusual in Victorian fiction (except in the underestimated novels of George Meredith). When the Sunbeam meets and falls in love with Face-of-god, she admits that she would sleep with him if he was to ask her to. He does not do so, recognising that it would dishonour her people, but the situation is openly presented and the heroine given a full range of feelings.

In 1890 Morris continued his work in fiction with *The Story of the Glittering Plain* (first published in the *English Illustrated Magazine*), and *News from Nowhere* (in *Commonweal*). In the former, which concerns the search of Hallblithe for his beloved who has been carried off by sea-rovers, the hero finds himself in a negative version of the earthly paradise, in which there are no conflicts but there is no real fellowship either. Hallblithe exclaims in resentment 'I seek no dream, but the end of dreams'. In view of the extent to which Morris's art had been sustained by the dream, this is a significant moment. No longer content with what in an earlier defeatist mood he had accepted as the only escape from harsh reality, Morris now seeks the transformation of society – and this despite the increasing tensions between himself and the anarchists within the League, and its failure to grow in numbers. In *News from Nowhere*, finally, he set himself to bring his dreams into the political world. How far did he succeed? Readers of the story must answer that question for themselves. They are perhaps no more likely to be agreed than two of the early reviewers. Lionel Johnson, the young poet, writing in *The Academy* found 'so much beauty, so much strength, so much sanity in a short book, that our thoughts of it must be thoughts of gratitude'. Maurice Hewlett, on the other hand, in a thorough discussion in the *National Review* entitled 'A Materialist's Paradise', attacked what he regarded as the antinomianism, the immorality, of the book, with its assumption that 'the good of the human race has been best served by indulging the appetites of its grosser parts and leaving the soul to find its level in a slough of sensuality and drowsy oblivion'.

The human imagination, refusing to be shackled by the present, has always played freely over past and future; Arcadia and Utopia, sinless worlds and perfect societies, embody man's dreams of what ought to be, and usually arise from a particularly vivid sense of the contrast between the ideal and the present reality. It is not surprising that Morris, with his distaste for the present and his romantic inheritance of the dream, should have turned to this kind of fiction as part of his involvement in socialism. He had long been an admirer of More's *Utopia,* and he was horrified by the picture of the future put forward in Edward Bellamy's very successful *Looking Backward,*[10] which he read in 1889. For the American Bellamy the society of the future could be comfortably envisaged as the industrial and commercial world of the Great Trust, administered from the centre by a highly efficient bureaucracy. Nothing could have been less attractive to Morris: 'Thank you. I wouldn't care to live in such a cockney paradise as he imagines', he wrote to Bruce Glasier. Soon he set about creating his own picture of an alternative society, which took shape as *News from Nowhere,* probably the best known now of all Morris's writings.

As it was first published in instalments in *Commonweal* and was intended for a popular audience, Morris wrote as simply and lucidly as he could. The vocabulary leaned to the Anglo-Saxon rather than the Latin, but did not far depart from contemporary usage, and the method of the dream-vision, familiar to Morris from much mediaeval literature, provided a clear basis on which to build. The structure is clear : the narrator goes home after a discussion of the future at a League meeting, his head buzzing with ideas, and goes to sleep in his house in Victorian Hammersmith; when he wakes the next day it is to a changed world, which he gradually discovers to be that of the future. The place is the same, but a revolution and subsequent developments have produced a society which puzzles but attracts him, and finding out about which provides the substance of the book. At first he is seen at the Guest House in Hammersmith (which bears a placard commemorating it as the former site of the lecture room of the Hammersmith Socialists), and travelling with a friendly guide, Robert Hammond, in the London area. In the next section he is taken to see the historian, Old Hammond, from whom he learns about the changes and how they occurred. And in the final section he travels with Robert and his wife Clara, and the intelligent and vivacious Ellen, up the River Thames, to join in the harvesting which takes place near what is recognised as Kelmscott Manor (see the frontispiece, illustration no. 1); from there the return can only be to the 'dingy Hammersmith' where the dream had begun. No reader would find any difficulty in following the story, and the geographical exactness of it all ties down the fantastic elements to a reality which is already known. Most Utopias are abstract and theoretical; Nowhere is England reborn.

The world described is attractive in a number of ways. Above all the narrator, who calls himself William Guest, is impressed by the pervasive sense of equality among all the people he meets. By contrast with the class-consciousness of Victorian society, and our own uneasy compromises, here is a world in which men and women accept one another on free and equal terms. Expressions are friendly and confident, conversations frank and sincere. The term 'neighbour', so freely used, is appropriate to the prevailing feelings; there is no British reserve in behaviour here. The women are as far as possible from the conventions of Victorian society. Their dress allows them to be active, and they participate in physical activities. The leading carver in a group met in Oxfordshire, for instance, is a woman, freely acknowledged as leader by the men. Moreover, physical touch is often employed by both men and women, as the inhibitions of convention no longer apply. Clara is seen looking at Robert fondly, seeing him in her mind's eye 'amidst the rhymed strokes of the scythes; and she looked down at her own pretty feet with a half sigh, as though she were contrasting her slight woman's beauty with this man's beauty'. Physical presence is acknowledged in a direct and unembarrassed way. Morris succeeds in conveying the sense of a society of free and equal citizens who enjoy one another's company and have no urge to give orders and exact obedience.

The second emphasised feature of this society, and one which strikes us particularly today, is the quality of the environment. Everywhere William Guest is surprised and delighted to find beauty and life. The buildings are described in a way which conveys their beauty without being too specific; it is the intangible quality of their relationship to the setting that is emphasised. For instance, the first houses Guest sees at Hammersmith are described as 'low and not large . . . they were mostly built of red brick and roofed with tiles, and looked, above all, comfortable, and as if they were, so to say, alive and sympathetic with the life of the dwellers in them'. This says a great deal which modern architects and town-planners seem too often to ignore. But it is not the buildings alone which are friendly; so is the natural environment. Gardens flourish everywhere, and the banks of the Thames have been restored to a beauty lost in the nineteenth-century triumph of the railways; bird-life is vigorous – kites, magpies, sparrow-hawks, a martin and a pair of ravens are noted on one day. Ellen expresses her feelings about this convincingly by drawing a contrast with the Victorian period :

> 'England is not big', said I, 'but it is pretty.'
>
> 'Yes,' she said, 'and don't you find it difficult to imagine the times when this little country was treated by its folk as if it were a characterless waste, with no delicate beauty to be guarded, with no heed taken of the ever fresh pleasures of the recurring seasons, and changeful weather, and diverse quality of soil, and so forth? How could people be so cruel to themselves?'
>
> 'And to each other,' said I.

Morris draws the contrasting beauty of Nowhere in a fine description of the 'resting-place on the Upper Thames' where the travellers stop on the third day :

A delicate spire of an ancient building rose up from out of the trees in the middle distance, with a few grey houses clustered about it; while nearer to us, in fact not half a furlong from the water, was a quite modern stone house – a wide quadrangle of one storey, the buildings that made it being quite low. There was no garden between it and the river, nothing but a row of pear-trees still quite young and slender; and though there did not seem to be much ornament about it, it had a sort of natural elegance, like that of the trees themselves.

Descriptions like these suggest how the land of England has become fit for men to live in. Human activities, like building, and natural elements combine to make a truly attractive and satisfying environment, very unlike that in which Morris and his contemporaries lived.

All this is made possible by the attitude of mind which Morris frequently alludes to in his characters and which constitutes the third major characteristic of Nowhere. This attitude is one which places the highest value on the ordinary experiences of life. It finds its most lyrical expression in the figure of Ellen, and in the words she speaks on seeing the old house – in fact, Kelmscott Manor :

She led me up close to the house, and laid her shapely sun-browned hand and arm on the lichened wall as if to embrace it, and cried out 'O me ! O me ! How I love the earth, and the seasons, and the weather, and all things that deal with it, that grow out of it – as this has done.'

This statement is the final expression of an attitude found in most of the characters, which Guest at first finds puzzling. In fact he remarks to Old Hammond that 'people putting in practice commonly this sense of interest in the ordinary occupations of life startles me'. Similarly, Hammond explains later, 'The spirit of the new days, of our days, has to be delight in the life of the world; intense and overweening love of the very skin and surface of the earth on which man dwells, such as a lover has in the fair flesh of the woman he loves . . .' And, as he goes on to say, this has led to the rebirth of art as the satisfaction of the human desire to contribute to the process of living. The ordinary people whom the travellers talk to have the same keen interest in 'all the little details of life: the weather, the hay-crop, the last new house, the plenty or lack of such and such birds, and so on; and they talked of these things not in a fatuous or conventional way, but as taking I say, real interest in them. Moreover, I found that the women knew as much about all these things as the men . . .' This is closely linked to the 'recovery of the arts of life' which makes the environment so attractive and is shown in details like the 'bread . . . of several different kinds, from the big, rather close, dark-coloured, sweet-tasting farmhouse loaf, which was most to my liking, to the thin pipe-stems of wheaten crust, such as I have eaten in Turin', which Guest finds at Hammersmith. This contrasts with the fact that before the revolution bread had ceased to be made locally, and 'came down with the newspapers by an early train from London'. That Guest remains very much a Victorian is shown by the fact that at the end he is still puzzled to hear Dick speaking enthusiastically about the change of the year:

> 'How strangely you talk,' said I, 'of such a constantly returning and consequently commonplace matter as the sequence of the seasons.' And indeed these people were like children about such things . . .

The narrator explicitly contrasts this with the attitude of his own time, 'in which the prevailing feeling amongst intellectual persons was a kind of sour distaste for the changing drama of the year, for the life of earth and its dealings with men. Indeed in those years it was thought poetic and imaginative to look upon life as a thing to be borne, rather than enjoyed.' A proper enjoyment of life is characteristic of Nowhere as we are shown it: ordinary living is not transcended but raised to a higher quality.

This emphasis by Morris on making a response to Nature and ordinary human experience central to one's outlook on life may strike modern readers as obvious, but reviewers' responses show that it was highly relevant. Lionel Johnson, for instance, wrote in *The Academy*:

> What Browning called 'the mere joy of living' becomes less valuable every day. Nowadays people seem to pride themselves upon having headaches of body and soul; to relish the sensitiveness of their nerves, their delicate and diseased condition. Effeminate persons give us sonnets upon nature, full of fantastic sentiments, and of refined phrases; but a twenty miles' walk or a sleep under the stars would be to them a painfully athletic exercise. Nor have they that loving and personal regard for the very earth itself, which Mr Morris so rightly prizes . . .

This suggests that Morris was right to treat the theme so explicitly; there was a tendency in late Victorian culture for those distressed by the results of industrialisation to turn away into a world of art totally unrelated to the facts of life; the most famous spokesman for the superiority of art to nature and life at the time was the brilliant and flamboyant Oscar Wilde. But Morris's attitude had positively anti-religious implications, which Maurice Hewlett spelled out at length in the *National Review*:

> In sober truth, the very pith of the scheme is materialistic, the humanism of a sensuous temperament which sees the beauty of appearance and is too indolent or too indifferent to look deeper . . . Animal love and animal beauty, 'the lust of the flesh, the lust of the eyes, and the pride of life', are very volcanoes, breeding eruption and riot; burning fiercely, they scorch, and may not always be quenched by being let loose.

The vehemence of this shows that Morris was challenging deeply held convictions within the Christian tradition. Hewlett was right to see Nowhere as the antithesis of a society in which a high value was attached to moral discipline, especially in regard to sexual morality, and to the transcendental assumption that there is another world more important than this one.

These three elements – free and equal relationships, regard

for the environment and full acceptance of everyday living – must appeal to many readers. But when we come to other aspects of Nowhere which underly these elements there is likely to be much more disagreement. The society shown is in very many ways a contrast with nineteenth-century England : there is no Parliament, no courts, no prisons, no law in any recognisable form, no religion, no money, no railways, no education in the formal sense, little machinery, no cities as we understand them, little respect for books or interest in theories. Marriage is a more open institution. Now all these departures from what was known to the Victorians remind us of how much our society is akin to theirs, and how far from Morris's ideals. The question that arises is whether this is because all societies must be to a large extent like ours, in which case Morris is a mere fantasist, or whether his account of the future has some closer relation to the possibilities of political and social action.

Morris's account gives two kinds of explanation of the situation in Nowhere, a comparatively full historical explanation, and some much more elusive economic suggestions. The historical aspect is covered in Old Hammond's conversation with Guest, and takes the longest chapter in the book, 'How the Change Came', and its successor, 'The Beginning of the New Life'. Considering that Morris's experience of political struggle was limited, though it included the experience of Bloody Sunday in 1887 which is briefly alluded to, his account is remarkably convincing. It is based on the Marxist analysis of how increased class hostility will lead to revolution, and accepts that there must be violence in the process of change. The idea of evolution to a classless society through the achievement of state socialism via Parliament is rejected as a cul-de-sac; the combined workers have finally to overthrow the power of the state, using the strike weapon. The process is justified by its result, the destruction of commercialism, which has made possible the society we are shown in Nowhere; Hammond explains :

'Nor would it have been destroyed otherwise; except, perhaps, by the whole of society gradually falling into lower depths, till it should at last reach a condition as rude as barbarism, but lacking both the hope and the pleasures of barbarism. Surely the sharper, shorter

139

remedy was the happiest?'

'Most surely,' said I.

'Yes,' said the old man, 'the world was being brought to its second birth; how could that take place without a tragedy?'

This unflinching acceptance of the necessity of revolution to achieve social change is obviously one of the most controversial points about *News from Nowhere*. Morris was writing before the Russian Revolution, which has led to the grand anticlimax of Soviet communism, a system in which the dictatorship of the proletariat gives little evidence of evolving into the fully classless society. How Morris would have reacted to Stalinism one can only guess, but his instinct for freedom was very strong. Interestingly it was Sydney Webb, who advocated progress by nationalisation, who also admired Stalin's Russia. The reader of *News from Nowhere* must give his own answer to the implied question whether social progress is dependent on revolution, or whether the revolutionary act destroys the values it sets out to establish. Would so freely decentralised a system be likely to evolve from a revolutionary beginning? Might it not be better able to develop from our own situation constitutionally?

The second area of explanation in *News from Nowhere* concerns the economic bases of the new society, and here Morris is certainly sketchy. The main activities which we see taking place are building, road-mending and harvesting, and we also hear of the lesser arts which provide the frugally beautiful utensils and tools of living. We meet a dustman, but do not see him at work; the same is true of a weaver. There is no pollution by smoke, but the explanation of this vast change is inadequate. There is a new form of energy, but that is all we are told :

'I see no smoke coming from the furnaces,' said I.

'Smoke?' said Dick, 'why should you see smoke?'

This is with reference to a 'banded-workshop' where people gather for convenience in pursuing crafts that need large-scale equipment like 'ovens and kilns and glass pots'. But Guest is told that power is not more available there than elsewhere : 'Why should people collect together to use power, when they can have it at places where they live, or hard by, any two or three of them; or any one, for the matter of that?' Later, Guest sees barges travelling on the Thames, 'going on their way without any means of propulsion visible to me'. Dick notices Guest's interest, and remarks 'That is one of our force-barges; it is quite as easy to work vehicles by force by water as by land'. Here Morris clumsily avoids further explanation:

> I understood pretty well that these 'force-vehicles' had taken the place of our old steam-power carrying; but I took good care not to ask any questions about them, as I knew well enough both that I should never be able to understand how they were worked, and that in attempting to do so I should betray myself, or get into some complication impossible to explain; so I merely said, 'Yes, of course, I understand.'

The curious reader is not likely to be satisfied with this, because it implies a hidden technological aspect to the society of which we see little other evidence, although there is reference during the harvesting – which is carried out entirely by hand – to the participation of 'many who lead sedentary lives, whom it would be unkind to deprive of their pleasure in the hay-field – scientific men and close students generally'. The contribution of these scientists to Nowhere is obscure. And in fact Morris is at his least convincing in his suggestion that a large population could be sustained in a society whose economic methods are all small-scale and labour-intensive. The 'great change in the use of mechanical force' is said to be responsible for the decentralisation, making it unnecessary for people to live in large industrial cities and so allowing them to move back to the more natural environment of the countryside. There is also the suggestion that in the more relaxed society of Nowhere our compulsive search for higher standards of living has ceased. There are no luxuries, and simple living is universally accepted.

The oversimplification which marks Morris's treatment of the economic theme – he clearly shares something of Dick's reproach to Bob for having 'muddled your head with mathematics, and with grubbing into those idiotic old books about political economy' – may be seen at a much less serious level in the fact that the whole of Guest's experience of Nowhere takes place in beautiful June weather; no single drop of rain falls, and the descriptions of the summer in the Thames Valley are among the most beautiful parts of the book. But in a utopian world we do not expect exact realism, and this criticism seems trivial. Moreover, Dick's remarks to Guest near the end show an awareness of the place of summer in the seasons :

> 'Now we are in a fit mood for dinner', said Dick, when we had dressed and were going through the grass again; 'and certainly of all the cheerful meals in the year, this one of harvest is the cheerfullest; not even excepting the corn-harvest feast; for then the year is beginning to fail; and one cannot help having a feeling behind all this gaiety, of the coming of the dark days, and the shorn fields and empty gardens; and the spring is almost too far to look forward to. It is, then, in the autumn, when one almost believes in death.'

That 'almost believes' suggests how strong was Morris's urge to deny the inexorable fact of death, the same urge that led him to try to create an ideal human society.

In replying to Dick's remarks, Guest notes something child-like in the attitude of the people of Nowhere in their 'exaggerated interest in the weather'. By the criticism Morris forestalls those who might complain of exactly this suggestion that the people of Nowhere lack full human stature, for instance in their lack of intellectual curiosity or moral complexity. There are several other references to child-likeness. At one point Clara takes Guest's hand 'as an affectionate child would', and Old Hammond maintains that 'it is the child-like part of us that produces works of imagination'. Guest awakens early one morning by Runnymede, and walking upstream and hearing the chub splashing 'felt almost back again in my boyhood'. It can be seen from this that Morris was trying to create a picture of a society pervaded by the finest feelings that can be derived from childhood: relaxation, confidence, enjoyment, naturalness. He certainly felt, with the Romantics like Blake and Wordsworth, that humanity had grown up all too completely, and needed to recover some of the psychic health which should be associated with the child. A good deal of twentieth-century thought has been along the same lines; hence that changed attitude by which parents often feel, not that they must help to change the children into adults as soon as possible, but rather that it is a privilege to share their children's childhood.

This is one example of the many ways in which *News from Nowhere* remains relevant and suggestive in our time. It is concerned with the problems of industrialism and commercialism which still preoccupy us today. Moreover, it is a well-managed work, and the last pages poignantly return the traveller to his own time. At several points Guest has felt pangs of concern about having to leave his companions, and he has always been haunted by memories of Victorian England. The moment in the church, however, when he suddenly discovers that he is becoming invisible to those present, is memorably described :

> I felt lonely and sick of heart past the power of words to describe. I hung about a minute longer, and then turned and went out of the porch again and through the lime-avenue into the road, while the blackbirds sang their strongest from the bushes about me in the hot June evening.

And the return is fittingly completed by the sight of the old farm-labourer, dirty and tired, whose gesture in touching his hat 'with some real good will and courtesy, and much servility' points to the final contrast with the open and equal manners of Nowhere. The last paragraphs face the question of what a dream like this can mean in practical terms. Morris's claim is that it can serve to hearten those struggling to improve their society, 'to build up by little and little the new day of fellowship, and rest, and happiness'. And his final words make an important distinction : 'Yes, surely! and if others can see it as I have seen it then it may be called a vision rather than a dream.'

This is a high claim to make, but it is justified by the book. This country, and many others, have surely moved in this century to some extent towards Morris's ideals of equal relationships, improved environment and humanistic concern for the quality of life. Whether further progress is possible without the political revolution which Morris believed in when he wrote his story is still a matter for debate, as is the possibility (not envisaged by Morris) that a revolution might defeat its own ends. But the attractiveness to many readers of Morris's Nowhere suggests that however unconvincing some of the details of his picture may be, he had a true vision which humanity would be the poorer for ignoring. *News from Nowhere* thus makes a fitting climax to the period of Morris's greatest political activity, and in its resolute idealism show how courageously he rose to the crises which were destroying the Socialist League.[11]

Most of the accounts of Morris in these years were written by political associates. F. S. Marvin recalled meeting him in Faulkner's rooms in University College, Oxford, while he was an undergraduate in 1883 and 1884:

> He was a picturesque, breezy-looking figure, with an air of the sea about him, but saying rather little, and always, as it seemed, with a very distant look in his eyes.[12]

Bruce Glasier heard him lecture for the first time in Glasgow on 14 December 1884 on 'Art and Labour':

> He was then fifty-one years of age, and just beginning to look elderly. His splendid crest of dark curly hair and his finely textured beard were brindling into grey. His head was lion-like, not only because of his shaggy mane, but because of the impress of strength of his whole front.[13]

Marx's friend and collaborator, Friedrich Engels, concerned about the ineffectiveness of the English socialists, and never very favourable to the English, was far less impressed. In a letter to Paul Lafargue of 20 March 1886 he referred to Morris and Bax as 'our two political innocents [nos deux bébés en politique]', and to Laura Lafargue on 13 September 1886 he wrote that 'Morris is a settled sentimental socialist'. When the anti-parliamentarians proved successful at the 1887 congress of the League Engels saw Morris as the stooge of the anarchists, saying of him that he 'hates everything Parliamentary like poison, is hopelessly muddle-headed, and as a poet is above science'.[14] However, Morris's own observations about the movement do not suggest naïveté. His comment about Bernard Shaw for instance, in a letter of 17 June 1887, is very sharp:

> Shaw was bad and languid, but also 'superior'. He has once again got a pocket full of conundrums which he pulls out from time to time: his real tendencies are toward individualist-anarchism.

And a letter to Dr John Glasse, with whom Morris stayed while speaking in Edinburgh in 1887, shows how carefully he had thought about the question of whether the League should aim at parliamentary representation:

> I admit, and have always admitted, that at some future period it may be necessary to use Parliament mechanically; what I object to is *dependency* on parliamentary agitation. There *must* be a great party, a great organisation outside Parliament actively engaged in reconstructing society and learning administration whatever goes on in the Parliament itself. This is in direct opposition to the view of the regular parliamentary section represented by Shaw, who look upon Parliament as *the* means; and it seems to me will fall into the error of moving heaven and earth to fill the ballot boxes with Socialist votes which will not represent Socialist *men*. However, let them try it. I don't care so long as the League exists with the other aim of getting the workmen to look after their own affairs and thereby building up the new society in the shell of the old one.[15]

The passage suggests a possible reason why Labour governments in England have not noticeably changed English society towards a socialist ethic and have allowed the *laissez-faire* ideal of free collective bargaining to survive. Recent attempts at local participation and involvement are more in line with Morris's thinking, as a complement to if not a replacement for parliamentary action.

The Socialist League was, however, continuing to decline in numbers and to become more divided in opinions. The conference of May 1890 saw the anarchists in command, with Morris and Henry Halliday Sparling, who had married the keenly socialist May, ejected from the editorship of *Commonweal,* which then went on to publish violent and inflammatory articles (still supported by Morris's money). The break came in November when the Hammersmith Socialist Society withdrew from the League, which declined into anarchistic violence stimulated by Auguste Coulon, who was in the pay of the police. It was a sad ending to an enterprise which had meant much to Morris and for which he had worked so hard. He took it with courage, writing to Bruce Glasier not to be downcast : 'It has been the curse of our movement that we lie to ourselves about progress and victories.' Morris moved into the final phase of his life with his idealism and his creative impulses still vital, though with a saddened recognition that progress must be a good deal slower than he had hoped.

6

The Last Stage, 1890–6

Morris remained a staunch socialist for the rest of his life, and worked to make the Hammersmith Socialist Society, founded on 23 November 1890, an effective propagandist force. To this end the series of Sunday evening lectures in the old coach-house adjoining Kelmscott House on the Mall, which had been inaugurated in 1884 by Hyndman and continued through the Socialist League days, was maintained. Many leading socialists spoke there, including Bernard Shaw, John Burns, Sidney Webb, Keir Hardy and Morris himself. The building itself was austere, as Bruce Glasier's account (corroborated by others) makes clear :

> It was a large room, with the floor raised three steps at the further end, forming a dais or platform with a side door leading into the garden of the house. It was quite simply furnished, and visitors who expected it, and it seems many did, to be fitted up as a sort of Morris art show-room were disappointed with its severely utilitarian character. The furniture consisted of rush-bottom chairs and several long wooden forms, a lecture table on the platform, and a bookstall near the entrance. The plain whitewashed walls were covered with rush matting.[1]

The audience consisted of local members of the Society together with visitors drawn by the reputations of the Sunday evening meetings – perhaps more of the latter in the later years when audiences could be as large as 200 people. Morris and Shaw were the two most regular speakers, and an account by Ernest Rhys in his autobiography *Everyman Remembers* vividly contrasts the two men, beginning with a description of Morris:

> How well as he stood up on the platform that Sunday night he fulfilled one's idea of a poet and leader of new causes! Of short, sturdy build, with noble head and shoulders that seemed designed for a much taller man, wearing his famous blue shirt and blue pilot coat, he looked like some valiant sea-captain on the deck of his ship. He was not what you may call a born speaker; he had a way of blurting out his sentences and some-times breaking off in the middle of one as if he was too impatient to finish it off. But his earnestness, his air of determined conviction, carried his hearers with him, or at least carried those who were sympathetic, for there was an opposition party in the hut who either resented his stepping out of the Middle Ages into the modern arena, or who thought him quite wrong as a tactician. However that might be, he put some restraint on himself while still reading his paper from a manu-script. It was afterwards, when Bernard Shaw had replied, and he rose again in his turn, that the excite-ment reached its head.
>
> Bernard Shaw as he stepped to the front of the platform made an absolute contrast to Morris. His sandy or reddish-yellow hair and coarse sandy whiskers framed a face that looked dead white as compared with Morris's florid complexion. He was much taller too, and his way of speaking was cool, collected, provocative. He seemed to take a pleasure in planting malicious little darts, or uttering taunts which roused Morris to something like humorous fury. The platform of the hut, I may say, had been hastily constructed and the planks were loose; and as Morris tramped up and down one feared at every moment they might collapse.

Also, he had an odd way as he glanced at his opponent
of thrusting his hands behind his back with an
awkward gesture, as if afraid he might be tempted to
make a personal attack upon the provoking, cynical,
plausible Irishman.

But at the end of the battle, the two combatants
went off together happily enough to sup at the poet's
house, followed by a group of other guests of whom I
considered myself lucky to be one.[2]

Other accounts confirm the contrast of personalities here
described by Rhys – including Shaw's own 'Morris as I knew
him'.[3]

Not surprisingly, the surviving accounts of the lectures express
varying attitudes towards them. Some, like Rhys and Bruce
Glasier, are largely favourable. Yeats, who was encouraged as
a young poet by Morris, writes warmly about him in his auto-
biographical *The Trembling of the Veil* (1922), and it was
evidently Morris's personality which brought him along since
he was never a socialist and was irked by the anti-religious
atmosphere of the meetings (Morris, characteristically, 'avoided
the subject altogether').[4] Other visitors viewed the occasions more
ironically. H. G.Wells, with his scientific outlook, came to view
his attendance as part of his 'earnest adolescence'; he recalled
'the grand head, the rough voice, the sturdy figure, sedulously
plain speech and lovable bearing of William Morris', but
dismissed him as an unrealistic political thinker : 'His dreamland
was not futurity, but an illuminated past.' Ford Madox Ford's
account in *Ancient Lights* (1911) is more sardonic, suggesting,
what can hardly have been the case, that most of the audience
consisted of young aesthetes such as he had been then. Elizabeth
Pennell in *The Life and Letters of Joseph Pennell* is more
thorough and thoughtful so that her criticisms have more point.
She writes : 'We found the Hammersmith service amusing as a
novelty, but not convincing as propaganda.' Her account of
Morris is vivid :

Morris was charmingly picturesque, short, sturdy,
bearded, in his blue reefer suit and blue shirt not unlike
a sea captain off duty. His thick curly hair was massed

about his forehead and always in confusion because of his habit of running his hands through it in moments of excitement and more often than not he was excited. He was weak in argument. In amiable mood, his retort to the straying sheep might be, 'My comrade does not believe it in his heart.' But as a rule, he lost his temper and said nasty things. At one long-remembered meeting he worked himself into the verge of apoplexy, calling his opponent every possible bad name, lost his voice in the process, and did not recover it all evening . . . The meetings grew monotonous, we went less often, gradually we were dropped. We were a disappointment to the comrades who had hoped to gather us into the fold. Even Morris wearied before long of his propaganda and was heard to say that, if he ever lectured again, it would be on the Norse sagas.[5]

When the next paragraph begins 'A distraction more to Pennell's taste was cycling' it is obvious that we are dealing with minds unable to attach to politics the importance it had come to hold for Morris; and the phrases 'we went less often, gradually we were dropped' seems to pass responsibility for what happened to the socialists rather than the Pennells, whose choice it was to cease attending. Nevertheless this passage draws attention to the limitation of the meetings as effective propaganda for socialism, as well as to the manic strain in Morris's personality. If his outbursts were comparatively few, this was not because self-restraint came easily to him; rather was it the result of much self-discipline.

No doubt Morris did become discouraged at times, especially by the tendency of early socialism to schism, so that he may have expressed a sentiment like that attributed to him about lecturing on the sagas; but in fact he never gave up lecturing and writing for socialism. The lectures of the last years were not brought together in his lifetime; some were published in a volume entitled *Architecture, Industry and Wealth* in 1902, and in the *Collected Works*, Vols. XXI and XXII. They cover both political and artistic subjects. A lecture 'On the Influence of Building Materials on Architecture' was originally delivered in 1892 to the Art Workers' Guild, one of a number of organisations which came into existence to co-ordinate the activities of the many craftsmen participating in what we now describe as the Arts and Crafts movement, the inspiration for which came to a large extent from Morris himself. The lecture is a significant reminder of the architectural basis of his thinking about art and society. It embodied principles which were widely ignored at a time when pride in the technological possibilities of materials was predominant – principles which the twentieth century has begun to acknowledge. Morris shows (in the account printed in the *Collected Works*, Vol. XXII from a reporter's notes of the informal address) his usual pleasure in the details of a craft, speaking for instance, of 'good bricks' with craftsman's relish. His final reflections on contemporary architecture remain to a disturbingly large extent valid today :

> I am afraid many of those we are building now will be looked upon as mere ingenious toys reflecting a good deal of credit perhaps on the intellect of those who designed them, but very little credit in their good sense and their solidarity. You will say that the man was very clever, but he had terrible difficulties to overcome, and he did in a way overcome them after all. But what he has produced, at the very best, is not a building which forms part of the living shell and skin of the earth on which we live, but is a mere excrescence upon it, a toy which might almost as well, except for the absolute necessity that the people should have a roof to cover them, have remained simply a nicely executed drawing in the architect's office. What we have to get rid of is especially and particularly that.

It is only recently that the ideal of 'keeping in keeping', with its implied respect for the appropriate building materials for a particular locality, has become fashionable in English architectural circles, though it inspired the Arts and Crafts architects like C. F. A. Voysey and, in the early years, Edwin Lutyens. How far it will affect the future architecture of England is a matter of time – though also of hope.

The directly political lectures of the period are certainly fewer; but all Morris's activities were reduced after a serious illness in the spring of 1891 which seriously affected his kidneys and made him thereafter have to husband his strength with care. The important article 'How I Became a Socialist' appeared in *Justice* for 16 June 1894 (a fact which indicates Morris's efforts in these last years to reunite the English socialist movement). The article is briefer than the lectures and gives a cogent account of his development. He makes clear that when he joined the movement he was 'blankly ignorant of economics', and that he took his new commitment seriously :

> [I] even tackled Marx, though I must confess that, whereas I thoroughly enjoyed the historical part of *Capital,* I suffered agonies of confusion of the brain over reading the pure economics of that great work. Anyhow, I read what I could, and will hope that some information stuck to me from my reading; but more, I must think, from continuous conversation from such friends as Hyndman and Scheu, the brisk course of propaganda meetings which were going on at the time, and in which I took my share.

Morris then looks back to try to explain how it was that someone like himself, with a comfortable middle-class background which meant that economic necessity was not painfully felt, should have been attracted to a radical ideal. He pays tribute to Carlyle and Ruskin as men who, at a period when most people accepted their civilisation with complacency or enthusiasm in 'the Whig frame of mind', set their voices against the age. Ruskin in particular taught him to 'give form to my discontent' and justify his 'leading passion . . . hatred of modern civilisation'. This leads Morris to an eloquent, but as usual unforced, meditation on the sterility and wastefulness of modern civilisation, ending in a striking rhetorical question :

> What shall I say concerning its mastery of and its waste of mechanical power, its commonwealth so poor, its enemies of the commonwealth so rich, its stupendous organisation – for the misery of life ! . . . Think of it ! Was it all to end in a counting-house on the top of a cinder-heap with Podsnap's drawing-room in the offing,

and a Whig Committee dealing out champagne to the rich and margarine to the poor in such convenient proportions as would make all men contented together, though the pleasure of the eyes was gone from the world, and the place of Homer was to be taken by Huxley?

The antithesis of Homer and the contemporary scientist T. H. Huxley is perhaps unfortunate in suggesting a simple romantic traditionalism on Morris's part, but the passage as a whole makes clear that Morris is repudiating modern civilisation in the name of a more generous and humane ideal. (Mr Podsnap in Dickens's novel *Our Mutual Friend* represents the complacent philistinism of the period which Morris, like Dickens, wished to sweep away.) A fierce egalitarianism comes out in the reference to champagne and margarine, and one feels that the 'Whig Committee' stands for all self-approving bureaucratic groups confidently organising society. The article ends with Morris's insistence that socialism must go beyond material progress, the achievement of all men of a 'decent livelihood', and so become involved with more inclusive cultural matters :

> It is the province of art to set the true ideal of a full and reasonable life before him [the workman], a life to which the perception and creation of beauty, the enjoyment of real pleasure that is, shall be felt to be as necessary to man as his daily bread, and that no man, and no set of men, can be deprived of this except by mere opposition, which should be resisted to the utmost.

This emphasis set Morris apart from the more purely economic socialism of Hyndman, and suggests the ideal of 'Socialism with a human face' as briefly preached in Czechoslovakia in 1968.

The lecture 'Communism' (1893) was reissued in 1903 as a Fabian Tract with a preface by Bernard Shaw and has subsequently become well known. In it Morris again emphasises the extent of his demands for the future by arguing that 'the great mass of what non-socialists at least consider to be socialism, seems to me nothing more than the machinery of socialism'. By this he has in mind such institutions as the London County Council, which substitutes 'business-like administration in the interests of the public for the old Whig muddle of *laissez-faire* backed up by coercion and smoothed by abundant corruption'. He also includes the municipal provision of parks and open spaces, and free libraries, and in the long term, the improvement of housing, working conditions and education. For he wants to go farther, towards a 'real society of equals'. This state of 'true and complete socialism' is what he calls communism, making a distinction which derives from Marx. He sees a danger that the 'machinery' so far considered might be used to shore up rather than replace the existing order. For him, this would be an inadequate response :

> The workers better treated, better organised, helping to govern themselves but with no more pretence to equality with the rich, nor any more hope of it than they have now. But if this be possible, it will only be so on the grounds that the working people have ceased to desire real socialism and are contented with some outside show of it joined to an increase in prosperity enough to satisfy the cravings of men who do not know what the pleasure of life might be if they treated their own capacities and the resources of nature reasonably with the intention and expectation of being happy.

This raises questions still highly relevant today, and not only in the West. How far have societies either under capitalism or under what is now called communism – not necessarily what Morris intended by the word – advanced towards the ideal he presents of a society of equals? And how far is it possible to go without interfering with social dynamics? Were Morris's ideals extravagant? What direction should society take now? Morris had no doubt about the answer to that question : 'I do declare that any other state of society but Communism is grievous and disgraceful to all belonging to it.'

Later in the lecture Morris admits that there has been a change in his own attitude since he had believed in 'the inevitableness of a sudden and speedy change'. He has come to take 'soberer views', recognising that the time is not yet ripe for revolutionary change. It is all the more necessary, then, to educate the working class into socialism so that 'they understand themselves to be face to face with false society, themselves the only possible elements of true society'. The 'machinery' will have proved of value if it acts as part of a development towards truly socialist aims. Morris tries to define these, stressing communal ownership of the resources of society, and production for use, not profit. He envisages a truly egalitarian society. His reply to the imaginary question 'How will you sail a ship in a socialist condition?' is :

> Why with a captain and mates and sailing master and engineer (if it be a steamer) and ABs and stokers and so on and so on. *Only* there will be no 1st, 2nd and 3rd class among the passengers : the sailors and stokers will be as well fed and lodged as the captain or passengers; and the captain and the stoker will have the same pay.

After this resolutely idealistic picture of the future, Morris concludes with an appeal to all socialists not to quarrel over the means if they agree about the desirable end :

> It is difficult or even impossible not to make mistakes about these [means], driven as we are by the swift lapse of time and the necessity for doing something amidst of it all. So let us forgive the mistakes that others make, even if we make none ourselves, and be at peace among ourselves, that we may then better make War upon the monopolist.

This is an attractively directed conclusion, though not without a neat reprimand to doctrinaire self-righteousness ('even if we make none ourselves'). Morris was now striving to build a united socialist movement, as his reconciliation with the SDF in 1894, and his support of George Lansbury as an SDF candidate for Parliament at Walworth in 1894 and 1895 suggests. His own role was to act as a spokesman for the ideal towards which more practical men were working more directly.

Perhaps this aim on Morris's part helps to account for the tone of *Socialism: its Growth and Outcome* which he and Belfort

Bax published in 1893, based on *Commonweal* articles of the previous year. Even *The Athenaeum,* by no means a radical journal, found it tame; nineteen chapters of familiar history followed by two of perfunctory concern with the 'outcome'. Of these the reviewer wrote :

> They might be sermons upon Socialism preached from a pulpit by one of the fashionable clergymen of the day in whom Socialism assumes its pleasant 'society' forms and who does not wish to drive away from his church the capitalists who support its institutions. The book will be read because it is so pretty and so pleasant, but we fear that it will not increase the sum of human knowledge.

This is a surprising Victorian response to a work which argued that violence, although not the main means of change, 'may be an *incident* in the struggle, and in some form or other probably will be, especially in the latter phases of the revolution'. Morris can seldom be accused of refraining from speaking out. If he was now trying to define carefully all the elements necessary for the revolution he believed in, he was still wholeheartedly committed to the attainment of a society of equals no matter how sharp the conflict might be with the defenders of privilege. His political writings in the 1890s are an important part of his achievement and show that he never abandoned his socialist principles.

Morris's most absorbing new activity proved to be the Kelmscott Press, established in 1890 in a house a few doors up the Mall in Hammersmith from Kelmscott House. From 'A Note by William Morris on his Aims in Founding the Kelmscott Press', dated 11 November 1895, can be discerned his thoroughness and care for detail :

> I began printing books with the hope of producing some which would have a definite claim to beauty, while at the same time they should be easy to read and should not dazzle the eye, or trouble the intellect of the reader by eccentricity of form in the letter . . . Looking at my adventure from that point of view then, I found I had

to consider chiefly the following things : the paper, the form of the type, the relative spacing of the letters, the words, & the lines, & lastly the position of the printed matter on the page.

Morris was helped and encouraged in his 'adventure' by his neighbour Emery Walker, who lectured to the Arts and Crafts Exhibition Society on printing in November 1888 and who was very knowledgeable on the subject. Morris entered into this activity with great enthusiasm, and immediately set about designing a typeface. He took as the model a fine face by Nicolas Jensen of 1476 and, with the aid of photograph enlargements, re-drew the alphabet to his own satisfaction. It was cut for him by Edward Prince, and trial pages were produced early in 1891. Morris called it the Golden type. In it appeared the earliest Kelmscott books, *The Story of the Glittering Plain* and *Poems by the Way*. Morris went on to design another type, a semi-blackletter of German origin which he preferred for more mediaeval books; it was called the Troy and, in its smaller size, the Chaucer. Many Kelmscott books had decorated initials and borders designed by Morris, while illustrations were mainly by Burne-Jones, but also by Walter Crane, C. M. Gere and Arthur Gaskin.

The speed of production was extremely rapid for a hand-press. In 1892 alone there appeared Wilfrid Scawen Blunt's *Love Lyrics and Songs of Proteus, The Defence of Guenevere, A Dream of John Ball,* Caxton's *Golden Legend* in three volumes, Caxton's *Recuyell of the Historyes of Troy,* J. W. Mackail's *Biblia Innocentium, News from Nowhere,* and a translation from the Dutch of *Reynard the Fox.* This pace was maintained until Morris's death, and indeed until the winding-up of the Press in 1898. Morris was able to print fine versions of works that he respected as well as many of his own works. Among those chosen were Thomas More's *Utopia,* poetry by Coleridge, Keats, Shelley, Tennyson, Rossetti and Swinburne, several mediaeval books and, most ambitiously of all, *The Works of Geoffrey Chaucer,* illustrated by Burne-Jones. The Kelmscott Chaucer, as it is known, is one of the most elaborate books ever produced. It was appropriate that Morris and Burne-Jones, who had admired Chaucer ever since their Oxford days, should have made the edition of him their final collaborative effort. The book was completed early in 1896; Burne-Jones wrote to F. S. Ellis about it in April:

> I have worked at it with love, and was almost as sorry as glad when the work was done; but, as you say, what praise shall be given to Morris; and who else could have carried it through, and who else have designed it as he has? A few more weeks now and it will be out, and I almost believe – so childishly hopeful am I – that as many as seven people will be delighted with it. I put it at a high number, but then I feel exhilarated.[6]

Burne-Jones's final comment raises an important question about these books, most of which formed expensive limited editions. Does it matter that they could in the nature of things have only a small circulation? Some of the products of the Press are far less elaborate, but the Chaucer itself, which gave Morris enormous pleasure, cannot be seen as a convenient reading edition; rather is it a craftsman's tribute to the mediaeval poet. However, artistic developments occur in oblique ways. The influence of the Kelmscott Press was far greater than might have been expected. It helped give impetus to a movement for improving book design which has been very influential throughout Western Europe and America. Modern books do not look like the products of the Kelmscott Press, but typographers like Stanley Morison who created the modern style have freely acknowledged the influence of Morris. For our taste his design may have been over-elaborate and the Troy type less legible than those we prefer, so that simpler books than the Chaucer appeal more; but his feeling for the proportions of the printed page were assured and his overall influence was profoundly beneficial.

The stained-glass work of the Firm continued in the 1890s, but by now it owed more to Burne-Jones than to Morris, and even Burne-Jones was more involved with other activities, especially painting and the design of tapestries. His figures for glass were of the elongated, dreamy, effeminate or emaciated type with which his reputation has become too much associated; his earlier work had been a good deal more forceful. Such figures can be seen in Albion Congregational Church, Ashton-under-Lyme, in the north and south transepts, where they contrast with the greater vitality of the east window of 1893 based on older cartoons. In St Margaret's, Rottingdean, the Sussex village where the Burne-Jones family now lived, similar figures appear in the chancel and the east window; there is more life in the smaller scenes below the main figures of the east window, the Annunciation, St Michael slaying the Dragon, and a Guardian Angel leading a Soul, which remind one of earlier work. The windows at Manchester College, Oxford (1895–9), make successful use of a number of the old designs, particularly the fine series of the Days of Creation, designed for Middleton Cheney in 1870. The most ambitious window of the period was for J. D. Sedding's Holy Trinity, Sloane Street, Chelsea. This is a large church, begun in 1888 in the Perpendicular style of the Gothic revival, with a vaulted interior and splendid fittings from the Arts and Crafts movement which Morris had done so much to inspire. The huge east window contains twelve main vertical lights with complex tracery above, and offers a great challenge to any designer concerned about unity and composition. In fact, however, no great effort seems to have been made to cope with the problems : there are simply forty-eight single figures in four tiers, and although a fine crucifixion appears centrally in the tracery above, it is too small to achieve a significant focus. The visitor is still impressed by the glass – as indeed by the whole interior which exemplifies the vitality of the late Victorian period – but many feel that a great opportunity has been missed. A. C. Sewter has argued that 'had Morris himself been as interested and as active in the work of his stained-glass studio in the 1890s as he was in the 1860s, the result at Sloane Street would have been very different'.[7]

Morris now left a good deal of the pattern-designing to J. H. Dearle at Merton Abbey, but he still produced a further ten wallpapers and one chintz, the attractive 'Daffodil'. The designs exhibit a more flowing structure than during the previous period, and make no use of the diagonal : the tendency is towards a swaying upwards movement, as in the 'Bachelor's Button' (1892); this is illustration no. 8. Now there is a recurrence of the more naturalistic treatment of the earliest designs, though combined with conventional elements. This is particularly effective in the Blackthorn (1892); here the vertical structure is rigid, but not the details of the flowers – of which no fewer than four appear in blue, red and yellow, in addition to the 'trellis' of the tiny white flowers of the thorn itself. The colouring is clear, with four well-distinguished shades of green, and the overall effect rich and vital. A whole room in such as paper would be overwhelming, but a single wall could be most effective. That the Firm's decorative schemes could attain lightness is suggested by *The Studio's* contemporary account of Stanmore Hall, Stanmore, the interior of which had recently been completed :

> The painted ceilings, both in the entrance hall and staircase, deserve study not because they are 'hand-painted', but because of their beautiful forms and dainty colours. The delicate tones, like those of embroidery on the white sills, are in shades of pinks, purples, tender greens and spring yellows, on a pale creamy ground, the whole bright yet light and with an aerial effect . . . The large ornament and bold forms Mr Morris delights in prove their power to blend into a perfect whole, elaborate, but in no way over-whelming.[8]

The last of Morris's designs, produced shortly before his death in 1896, as both wallpaper and printed textile, was made for Compton Hall in Staffordshire, and is called 'Compton'. It fittingly exhibits Morris's inexhaustible sympathy with the English countryside, together with his powers of composition, as the leaves and flowers combine with undiminished freshness.

Morris's literary activities included the publication of his last volume of poetry, *Poems by the Way,* in 1891. The volume brought together most of the short poems he had written in the last twenty or so years, arranged in no obvious order. Some like 'Hope Dieth : Love Liveth' and 'Love Fulfilled' date back to the period of the *Earthly Paradise;* many reflect Morris's Nordic interest, including a series of translations of 1870–1 including 'The Lay of Christine' and 'Hafbur and Signy'; ten of them relate to paintings or tapestries, including the series 'For the Briar Rose'; there are six of the socialist songs which Morris wrote for the League; three sections of 'The Pilgrims of Hope'; and a few recent poems. Of these, 'Mine and Thine', translated from the mediaeval Flemish, neatly expresses the aspiration for a just, non-acquisitive society in unpretentious couplets. It looks forward to a time when possessiveness will have disappeared, concluding:

> Yea, God well counselled for our health,
> Gave all this fleeting worldly wealth
> A common heritage to all
> That men might feed them therewithal,
> And clothe their limbs, and shoe their feet
> And live a simple life and sweet
> But now so rageth greediness
> That each desireth nothing less
> Than all the world, and all his own;
> And all for him and him alone.

The other recent poems are more in the mode of the prose romances he was now writing, dealing with strange adventures in a distant world, but presented with fresh directness. 'The Folk-Mote by the River' has some of the qualities of a ballad, especially the sudden opening:

> It was up in the morn we rose betimes
> From the hall-floor hard by the row of limes
>
> It was but John the Red and I
> And we were the brothers of Gregory . . .

Here Morris employs the more rapid anapaestic rhythm which he preferred for contexts of action, and the poem moves rapidly into its story. The townsfolk of an unnamed town gather for the meeting of the community – folk-moot, in the Old English phrase. The scene is evoked with characteristic feeling for the countryside, amid the 'lime-boughs sweet' near the 'prattling weir'. The banners of the Freemen appear and the people gather: they are addressed by an elder in the tones of John Ball:

> For tell me, children, who are these?
> Fair meadows of the June's increase?
>
> Whose are these flocks, and whose the neat [cattle],
> And whose the acres of the wheat? . . .

Whose thralls are ye, hereby that stand,
Bearing the freeman's sword in hand?

It becomes clear that these men are in rebellion against their feudal master, who is demanding their surrender. The elder's scorn for the Earl Hugh is shared by the people, who are then addressed by Gregory the Wright [carpenter], father of the narrator. He names all the other groups who may join in the rising, and calls on the people to follow, which they do with 'shouts both glad and strong'. The ending recounts both the cost and the achievement of victory :

> And sooth it is that the River-land
> Lacks many an autumn-gathering hand.
>
> And there are troth-plight maids unwed
> Shall deem awhile that love is dead;
>
> And babes there are to men shall grow
> Nor ever the face of their fathers know.
>
> And yet in the land by the River-side
> Doth never a thrall or an earl's man bide;
>
> For Hugh the Earl of might and mirth
> Hath left the merry days of Earth;
>
> And we live on in the land we love,
> And grudge no hallow Heaven above.

The earth has been made fit for men's enjoyment and so they need not set all their hopes on futurity. Morris had enjoyed writing in the ballad manner and about mediaeval subjects from the days of 'The Haystack in the Floods' and 'Concerning Geffray Teste Noire'; the contrast with the earlier poems is in the more confident social philosophy that now finds expression, although the suffering necessary to achieve the ideal is not ignored.

If 'The Folk-Mote' recalls *John Ball* and *The House of the Wolfings*, 'Goldilocks and Goldilocks' suggests the more romantic atmosphere and mood of the stories of the 1890s. It also is written in couplets and has a rural setting, but its world (as the young hero's name, Goldilocks, suggests) is close to fairytale. The hero sets out briskly for no clearly defined purpose :

> The morn is fair and the world is wide,
> And here no more I will abide.

In the context we feel that Goldilocks is embarking on the quest of self-knowledge, for this kind of writing readily takes us into a world of myth and archetype. Goldilocks leaves the Upland Town and comes to the wild-wood; on the seventh morn he meets, and kisses, a 'sweet-mouthed maiden' with a voice 'sweet as the song of the summer bird'. Her name too, by a fairytale coincidence, is Goldilocks:

> He spake, 'Love me as I love thee,
> And Goldilocks one flesh shall be.'

They are clearly destined for each other. But of course the story, like all romances, must involve the overcoming of trials, and problems soon occur. However, these are eventually resolved by courage and love. The final words are spoken by the Swain as he contemplates the future:

> 'Come, love, and look on the Fathers' Hall,
> And the folk of the kindred, one and all!
>
> For now the Fathers' House is kind
> And all the ill is left behind.
>
> And Goldilocks and Goldilocks
> Shall dwell in the land of the Wheaten Shocks.'

It is an extremely well-managed poem, showing how naturally it came to Morris to use the forms and themes of mediaeval romance. It successfully elaborates, in its clear and simple way, the processes of nature and human love. In the rendering of the love Morris is again un-Victorianly outspoken: when Goldilocks stands beside her love at the end of the poem we are told that 'he saw her body sweet and good'. For Morris, whatever his personal experiences, the ideal of human love was of a natural and unashamedly sexual kind.

Poems by the Way was not widely reviewed, but did receive some favourable notices. No doubt it was the publication of the volume which led to Morris's name being raised in connection with the office of Poet Laureate, when Tennyson died in October 1892, having held the office ever since 1850. Since Browning and Arnold were both dead, and the poetry of Hopkins and Hardy very little known, Swinburne and Morris were the two obvious contenders. Swinburne had professed republican sentiments in his youthful verse, which seemed to make him as inappropriate as the socialist Morris. *The Bookman* published a symposium on the laureateship in November 1892 which included the remark :

> Mr Swinburne has hardly so entirely forgotten his lines about 'a linnet chirping on the wrist of kings' as to take an office directly from the Court; nor would Mr William Morris be ready to exchange lectures at Kelmscott House for songs about royal marriages, no matter how large a hogshead of sherry were made over to him in the bargain.[9]

This latter judgement is borne out by Mackail's report that a member of Gladstone's Cabinet did sound Morris out about the office, but that Morris made it clear that he could not be considered. In view of his revolutionary politics, the idea is indeed absurd : Morris never seems to have shared the common English liking for rank and title. He apparently thought it likely that the post would be offered to Swinburne and that he would accept it;[10] but in fact no appointment was made until 1896, when the office went to the critic and minor poet Alfred Austin.

Morris's writings at this period include some further translations. The ambitious *Saga Literary* was produced in conjunction with Eirikr Magnusson, the first volume in 1892 and running in all to six volumes. The scale of the work is a fitting reminder of the depth of Morris's enthusiasm for Icelandic literature. The Kelmscott Press also issued his translations from the French of four mediaeval stories, 'Of King Flores and the Fair Jehane' (1893), 'Of the Friendship of Amis and Amile' (1894), 'The Tale of the Emperor Constans and of Over Sea' (1894) – the last being two stories. When the group appeared as *Four French Romances* in 1896, the *Saturday Review* used a parodic method of review :

Now Master William Morris, being a right good maker, having erstwhile much good heirs of his celle fantastic, which were dainty of body and fashion, did add this hereto, that he did do unto the English of the street clept Wardour yet three much fair tales of France. So the said tales were done . . .

Some of the sentences quoted from the translation would justify such criticism if they were typical; Morris sometimes used an excessively 'mediaeval' style for his translations. He certainly went so far in his version of the Anglo-Saxon poem *Beowulf* (translated with the aid of the Oxford scholar A. J. Wyatt and published in 1895) that many readers find the translation almost as difficult to understand as the original. Fortunately the language of the contemporary prose romances, though deliberately archaic, never appears so strange.

In these prose romances, which constituted the main literary achievement of his last years, Morris showed himself against the age in his use of a form of fiction antithetical to the fashionable naturalism of the 1890s, shown most powerfully and grimly in the novels of Gissing with their emphasis on the sordid realities of everyday life among the genteel or industrial poor. It was Zola in France who had inaugurated this development with his belief in 'The Experimental Novel' based on an analogy with scientific experimentation. Oscar Wilde expressed a hostile view of naturalism through Vivian's outburst in his entertaining essay 'The Decay of Lying' in 1889:

'Mr Ruskin once described the characters in George Eliot's novels as being like the sweepings of a Pentonville omnibus but M. Zola's characters are much worse. They have their dreary vices, and their drearier virtues. The record of their lives is absolutely without interest. Who cares what happens to them? In literature we require distinction, charm, beauty and imaginative power. We don't want to be harrowed and disgusted with an account of the doings of the lower orders.'[11]

Morris would have been unhappy about the feeling of social superiority in this last remark, but not about the line of argument.

His preference had always been for something like the romance form of narrative, in which heroes and heroines set out on quests which suggest archetypal human needs in an imaginative world remote from the present. But his early stories in this mode had lacked the optimism which is usual in the genre, in which the happy ending is conventional. With his commitment to socialism, however, there came a renewed confidence in the ability of man eventually to liberate himself from the inequalities and injustices of existing types of society, and to achieve the 'society of equals'. This new optimism finds expression in Morris's confident use of the romance form towards the end of his life. In these stories there is less of the historical element of *The House of the Wolfings;* we cannot place them in any particular time or place. Nevertheless they can convey, through the adventures of their central characters, a clear sense of values which relates to Morris's most deeply held beliefs.

The earliest, *The Wood Beyond the World,* seems to have been begun in 1892, but was not published until 1894. A facsimile of the original Kelmscott Press edition is now available,[12] which enables the reader to experience something like the total effect at which Morris was aiming, one in which the onward movement of the narrative is set against an encouragement to dwell in a leisurely way over every appealing detail of the text; see illustration no. 7. Since the prose style of the romances has been seriously criticised for its quaintness and archaism, said to be allied to the escapist suggestions of the subject-matter, it is appropriate to examine a passage near the opening of the story in some detail :

> Now ye may well deem that such a youngling as this was looked upon by all as a lucky man without a lack; but there was this flaw in his lot, whereas he had fallen into the toils of love of a woman exceeding fair, and had taken her to wife, she nought unwilling as it seemed. But when they had been wedded some six months he found by manifest tokens, that his fairness was not so much to her but that she must seek to the foulness of one worser than he in all ways; wherefore his rest departed from him, whereas he hated her for her untruth and her hatred of him; yet would the

sound of her voice, as she came and went in the house,
make his heart beat; and the sight of her stirred desire
within him, so that he longed for her to be sweet and
kind with him, and deemed that, might it be so, he
should forget all the evil gone by. But it was not so; for
ever when she saw him, her face changed, and her
hatred of him became manifest, and howsoever she
were sweet with others, with him she was hard and
sour.

Clearly Morris is using language in a very different way from
Gissing, because he wants to take the reader at once into an
imaginative realm, rather than to confront him with the world
of ordinary experience. The diction – which has excited so much
criticism – is chosen for this end. In these paragraphs the idio-
syncratic elements are : ye may . . . deem; youngling; without
a lack; whereas (= because); exceeding fair; she nought
unwilling; wedded; seek to; worser; wherefore; untruth; howsoever. A consistent feature throughout the romances is the use
of the second person singular, especially in dialogue – a common
enough usage in authors aiming at a non-modern effect. The
diction is remarkable for the purity of its Old English emphasis.
Morris avoids words deriving from Latin or French when
Teutonic equivalents are available, and succeeds to a remarkable
extent in demonstrating his version of what R. C. Trench had
envisaged in a chapter of his *English, Past and Present* in 1855
entitled 'English as It Might Have Been' without the Norman
Conquest. None of the words used is obscure or difficult for the
modern reader, with the possible exception of 'whereas' used in
the sense of because. Some remind one of the Authorised Version
of the Bible; a few, usually those adapted from a familiar word,
like 'youngling' and 'seek to', suggest an extravagant determination to avoid conventional verbal forms. But it is misleading to
suggest that such elements predominate in the diction. Moreover,
this kind of criticism ignores an equally significant element in
the prose style, the predominance of monosyllables. In sample
passages analysed, Morris achieved something like 80 per cent
of monosyllabic words, a higher proportion than in other works
of a similar kind. Even if statistical estimation is unreliable
without extension to whole works, the reader is surely aware of

the basic simplicity of the style, which derives from the high number of monosyllables and the straightforward syntax. Some sentences are long, but these usually consist of a number of parallel clauses rather than exhibiting complex syntax; semi-colons are particularly numerous, and relationships are usually expressed by the simplest conjunctions (and, but yet) or relatives. This helps to create a sense of direct movement, in which the narrator is felt to be firmly in command of his material, which he presents in this clear and methodical way and in a mainly chronological sequence. Thus the reader who persists with the story after the first few paragraphs finds that there is a sustained thrust in the monosyllabic style which is appropriate to the succession of adventures of which the story consists. It is unfair to Morris's achievement in the romances to note the elements of archaism in the diction as if these superseded other elements of style.

In the story Golden Walter eventually defeats the evil forces represented by an ugly dwarf and his deceptively beautiful mistress, and is united with the simple Maid. (The fact that she is given no name reminds us that we are in a world of myth and archetype, representative figures rather than individual characters.) Walter passes the tests necessary to show himself fit to rule the town of Starkwell, and the Maid to be his consort, and the 'days of the Kingship' end the story in prosperity and justice. It was a review of *The Wood Beyond the World* which sought to interpret the story as an allegory of the relationship between capital and labour which led Morris to write to the *Spectator* in July 1895:

> I had not the least intention of thrusting an allegory
> into *The Wood Beyond the World;* it is meant for a
> tale pure and simple, with nothing didactic about it. If
> I have to write or speak on social problems, I always
> try to be as direct as I possibly can.

This may suggest that we should avoid trying to see any general significance in Morris's stories. But what is 'a tale pure and simple'? Is it one from which no conclusions about human nature or behaviour can be drawn? Perhaps the discrimination is not as clear as Morris suggests. Although it is absurd to try to interpret the romances in a precise allegorical way, there is no reason to ignore the deeper implication of the characters' behaviour, the respect for effort, courage and achievement, and the celebration of social cohesion.

It is impossible to examine all the romances in depth; so concentration now will be on the most elaborate of them, *The Well at the World's End*, published in 1896 though written earlier. It is primarily the story of Ralph, the youngest of the four sons of King Peter of Upmeads. When his three brothers go off to seek adventure as the result of drawing lots, Ralph goes too, despite having lost. In the story his boldness is justified, and he ends a greater man than the brothers. In seeking adventure he hears of the Well and decides that he will drink of its waters, which are said to have supernatural powers. He has a passionate love affair with the enigmatic Lady of Abundance, which ends dramatically with the arrival of her husband, the Knight of the Sun :

> He turned at once upon Ralph, shaking his sword in the air (and there was blood upon the blade) and he cried out in a terrible voice : 'The witch is dead, the whore is dead ! And thou, thief, who hast stolen her from me, and lain by her in the wilderness now shalt thou die, thou !'

These events add an unexpected and disastrous end to what had been a courtly affair; Ralph shoots the Knight dead with an arrow, but the Lady dies in his arms. Now alone in the world, Ralph's thoughts are 'of his home at Upmeads, which was so familiar to him, and of the Well at the World's End, which was but a word'. These are the two poles of the story, and of Ralph's experience. He now journeys on towards the Well, through traditional adventures of war and travel, including becoming a prisoner of the tyrannical Lord of Utterbol in his grim and exploited country.

Soon after starting on his adventures, Ralph had met a simple girl, Ursula, whom he then regarded with brotherly affection. As he journeys on, he hears news of the girl, who has also left home and now become a captive in Utterbol. With the inevitability of the romance story, they meet again when both escape their captors, and proceed together towards the Well. invention of suggestive place names: 'They come to the Sea of Swevenham. The chapter-headings show Morris's skill in the invention of suggestive place names: 'They come to the Sea of Molten Rocks', 'They come to the Gate of the Mountains', 'They come to the Vale of Sweet Chestnuts'. In this place they pass the winter, and become aware of physical attraction towards each other. But their relationship is contrasted with that between Ralph and the Lady, which had been based on passion; now Ursula suggests that they should wait to consummate their love until there can be witnesses to the marriage, and Ralph agrees – though not without insisting on 'such kissing and caressing as is meet between troth-plight lovers'. They do not have long to wait, but the point has been made that love should not be merely passion but should involve a sense of social responsibility. Now the pair can move on through the Land of the Innocent Folk and the Woodland to the Thirsty Desert, in which they find the bodies of many dead seekers of the Well. Next they come to the Dry Tree, which stands paradoxically in 'a pool of clear water', with its branches displaying helmets, swords and spears. Ralph wants to drink from the pool, but is dissuaded by Ursula; a crow which drinks falls dead at their feet. The scene becomes more dramatic:

> Then she looked in Ralph's face, and turned pale and said hastily, 'O my friend, how is it with thee?'
> But she waited not for an answer, but turned her face to the bent [hillside] whereby they had come down, and cried out in a loud, shrill voice: 'O Ralph, Ralph! look up yonder to the ridge whereby we left our horses; look, look! There glitters a spear and stirreth! and lo a helm underneath the spear: tarry not, let us save our horses!'
> Then Ralph let a cry out from his mouth, and set off running to the side of the slope, and fell to climbing it with great strides, not heeding Ursula; but she followed close after, and scrambled up with foot and hand and knee, till she stood beside him on the top, and he looked round wildly and cried out: 'Where! where are they?'
> 'Nowhere', she said, 'it was naught but my word to

draw thee from death; but praise be to the saints that
thou art come alive out of the accursed valley.'

It would seem that Ursula as a woman is gifted with a quality
of insight which the male hero does not possess. It is Ralph and
Ursula together who are capable of reaching the Ocean-Sea and
the Well. They drink from the golden cup with the inscription
'The Strong of Heart still Drink from Me', Ralph crying out,
'To the Earth, and the World of Manfolk !' They linger for a
while in the beautiful garden by the Well which is compared
to the Garden of Eden :

> And the deer of that place, both little and great, had
> no fear of man, but the hart and hind came to Ursula's
> hand; and the thrushes perched upon her shoulder,
> and the hares gambolled together close to the feet of
> the twain; so that it seemed to them that they had
> come into the very Garden of God . . .

But unlike Adam and Eve, they do not have to be expelled from
the garden. In accordance with Morris's convictions about
human responsibility, they leave of their own accord to return to
Ralph's home country.

The importance of the return is clear from the fact that it
occupies a quarter of the story. The journey neatly traverses
much of the ground they had covered earlier, but with striking
changes. Utterbol has a new ruler, an old friend of Ralph who
has killed the tyrant and established freedom and justice. Now
rumours begin to reach them that all is not well at Upmeads,
and this proves to be true. King Peter has left the country because
of invasion by the Burg-men. Ralph raises a great army and
marches into his homeland. When the Burgers send out their
challenger, Ralph is seen at his most magnificent : 'his head was
bare, for now he had done off his sallet, and the sun and the
wind played in his bright hair; glorious was his face, and his grey
eyes gleamed with wrath and mastery'. The challenger retires,
discomfited, and the great battle that follows Ralph's coming
is triumphant. Ralph can now bring his father and mother back
to Upmeads, where the father abdicates in favour of Ralph, the
greater leader. Ursula is accepted as queen, despite her lowly

birth, and the people of Upmeads can live in peace and security: 'it is told of Ralph of Upmeads that he ruled over his lands in right and might, and suffered no oppression within them, and delivered other lands and good towns when they fell under tyrants and oppressors . . . and no lord was ever more loved'. As is usual in Morris's romances, the ending is both a home-coming and an affirmation of social justice.

The Well at the World's End thus embodies beliefs very dear to Morris in the attractive form of a romance. In the sign of the Sword and the Bough, by which Ralph and Ursula are guided to the Well, can be seen a neat image of Morris's funda-mental values. The Sword represents the active, masculine side of the personality – there was nothing of the pacifist in Morris's make-up – the belief that courage and effort are needed if good is to prevail over evil. Early in the story Ralph comes to the town of Higham, which is ruled by a warrior Abbot. While there he talks to a monk, who warns him that in journeying in the world he is likely to experience suffering:

> Then came a word into Ralph's mouth, and he said: 'Wilt thou tell me, father, whose work was the world's fashion?'
>
> The monk reddened, but answered nought, and Ralph spoke again: 'Forsooth, did the craftsman of it fumble over his work?'
>
> Then the monk scowled, but presently he enforced himself to speak bitterly, and said: 'Such matters are over high for my speech or thine, lord; but I tell thee, I who know, that there are men in this house who have tried the world and found it wanting.'
>
> Ralph smiled, and said stammering: 'Father, did the world try them, and find them wanting maybe?'

Here any ideas of monastic seclusion and escapism are explicitly rejected, which makes it less convincing to charge the romances in general with this tendency. They avoid contemporary society, only to point to the value of action in the world at any time. Morris and Burne-Jones had thought as undergraduates of founding a monastic order; now Morris advocates direct involve-ment with the world through the symbol of the Sword.

The complementary symbol of the Bough represents the side of Morris which informs his designs and the descriptive passages in many of his poems and stories. Man, it is implied, must learn to live in harmony with nature and himself. This involves the acceptance of the gentler, feminine side of the personality – though it should be noted that the heroines of the romances are physically active and determined people, with a freedom of action which Victorian women notably lacked. In *The Wood Beyond the World* this spirit is beautifully expressed when the Maid demonstrates to the men of the Bear that she is the spirit of summer as 'the breeze that came up the valley from behind bore the sweetness of her fragrance all over the Man-mote'. In *The Well at the World's End* the Bough is associated closely with the Well itself, and vividly by contrast with the Dry Tree. Life-giving water is the basis of nature's fecundity, and those who drink of the Well then ally themselves with the processes of nature. In the garden by the Well Ralph and Ursula 'forget all the many miles of the waste and the mountain that lay before them, and they had no thought for the strife of freemen and the thwarting of kindred, that belike awaited them in their own land, but they thought of the love and the happiness of the hour that was passing'. Ralph's toast had been 'To the Earth, and the World of Manfolk!' It would be inconsistent with Morris's acceptance of man's place in nature to allow great importance to the supernatural. Thus the Maid has to return to the men of the Bear and tell them that she was not a goddess but a woman, and Ralph and Ursula, despite drinking from the Well, must die. They are preserved from ageing, but not from death: 'On one day they two died and were laid together in one tomb in the choir of St Laurence of Upmeads.' The natural cycle must be accepted by those who respect the Earth and the symbol of the Bough.

Morris wrote three further romances; *Child Christopher and Goldilind the Fair* was inspired by the reading of the fourteenth-century English 'Lay of Havelock the Dane'. The struggle of the hero and heroine to retrieve their rightful realms from evil men becomes successful when they are united; again Morris emphasises the necessity for wholeness of being to overcome selfishness and greed. *The Water of the Wondrous Isles* begins unusually in the sordidness of Victorian London, but moves on

to deal mainly with Birdalone's search for freedom and fulfilment. *The Sundering Flood,* which Morris was dictating until
a short while before his death, is unrevised, but nevertheless
complete. Here the interest is as much in the earth as in the
characters, and again the idea of the unity both of man and
woman and of humanity with nature is central. Near the end
there is a brief scene between Steelhead and a hermit which
reminds one of the argument with the monk in *The Well at the
World's End* as well as suggesting a personal application to the
dying Morris:

> 'Go in peace, and God and Allhallows keep thee,' said
> the hermit.
> 'Well, well,' said Steelhead, 'we will not contend
> about it, but I look to it to keep myself.' And therewith
> he strode off into the night.

Morris's view is humanistic; if there is any force beyond men
themselves, it is to be glimpsed in nature, not in some trans-
cendent God. An Icelandic acceptance is the final note.

An anonymous reviewer of *The Sundering Flood* in *The
Academy* in March 1898 raised very clearly the basic critical
issue about all the romances. The reviewer argued that the story
had a good deal of charm which might make it, in simpler
language, suitable for children, but felt that it had no further
value:

> The author had a quick and sure eye for any fair vision
> of men and women, but never did he master that
> essential of all great novels, the effect produced on
> character by the shocks and blows of circumstance.
> Barring that his lovers add a few feet to their stature
> and a few pounds to their weight, they are at the end
> what they were at the beginning, as wise and not a
> whit less virtuous. And where this is so it is obvious that
> the wildest adventure has no more literary value than
> an exciting paragraph in a daily paper.

Explicit here is the belief that the psychological development of
characters is the proper stuff of fiction. This became a common

assumption because of the great achievements of the realistic novel in the nineteenth century. Certainly in George Eliot and Henry James we find precisely what the critic is asking for. But his remarks are less apposite to Dickens, whom Morris admired more than any other novelist except Scott, and raise the question why there cannot be various equally valid types of fiction of which the realistic novel is only one. Twentieth-century developments have been along these lines, with departures from realism of many kinds, the most popular being the development of science fiction. In view of such developments and the enormous success of Tolkien's *The Lord of the Rings,* it is now possible to see Morris's romances not as failed realistic novels, but as unusual and interesting creative fiction of their own kind.

An external observer's impression of Morris in the 1890s comes from the French writer Gabriel Mourey, who contributed the 'Gil Blas' column about English culture to *Figaro* in Paris. His articles were brought together as *Passé le Detroit* in 1895, and translated into English the following year as *Across the Channel. Life and Art in London.* Morris appears under the heading, 'Renaissance of Industrial Art' and a physical description comes first :

> The complexion is ruddy, the hair, greyish in hue, short and curly. He is of medium height but powerfully built, a true northern physique, and there is about him the attractiveness of those heroic conquerors of whom northern legends tell, and of whom he is so fond. He is a mixture of that hesitating brusqueness peculiar to the timid, of that reticence and coldness of the man who is intensively reserved and opposed to all display of personal feeling. These traits are interspersed with sudden transports of kindness, fits of enthusiasm which seem to kindle his whole being, to lift him to heights beyond, and to transfigure him.[13]

Mourey describes a visit to Kelmscott House, with Morris working on the Chaucer, while on the table are 'piles of proof-sheets, patterns of cretonnes and velvets from Merton Abbey, papers covered with painted designs in process of preparation'.

Morris talks, particularly about printing, and about the influence of mediaeval art on him. Mourey then goes on to discuss Morris's influence on English taste, which he considers 'deep and restorative', and to be discerned on all sides – 'in bar and restaurant, in the decoration of fireside and theatre lobby, in the halls of those fine houses in Kensington and Chelsea, in studios, and in the parlours of small middle-class houses'. Above all Mourey feels in Morris 'a touch of the religious austerity of fervour of his first intended vocation', now 'bestowed upon a human cause' in the earnestness of his commitment to 'humanitarian and socialist ideas'. Finally he recalls the atmosphere of the Merton Abbey works as bringing the natural environment into the life and activities of the worker. Mourey's account suggests how deeply Morris's personality could affect and impress a sympathetic observer in these years.

Burne-Jones, alerted by Morris's illness to the value of exact reminiscence, regretted his lack of accurate recall of spoken words:

> 'There's Morris: the larger half of that wonderful personality will perish when he dies. I've tried to put down or repeat some of his rare sayings, but somehow they seemed flattish the day after, with the savour gone. There is no giving the singularity and independence of his remarks from anything that went before. What never can be put down are his actions and ways – perpetually walking about a room while he is talking, and his manner of putting his fist out to explain the thing to you. When I first knew him at College it was just what it is now.'[14]

Any great man of the past leaves the modern reader with a sense of deprivation, since we cannot see him alive again. Fortunately the records of witnesses and friends can help to restore for us a sense of the personality, while the works survive as witnesses of another equally authoritative kind. In 1896 it became increasingly clear that Morris was seriously ill. Burne-Jones noted that on Sunday at breakfast at the Grange Morris had to lean his forehead on his hand – 'It is a thing I have never known him do before in all the years I have known him'.[15] He was losing weight and sleeping badly, and could work for shorter and shorter periods. Medical advice sent him to Folkestone in June, and on a voyage to Norway at the end of July, but neither helped. By late August he was back at Kelmscott House. In his weakness, he was given great pleasure by being shown mediaeval manuscripts and by the attendance of his family and many friends. He died in the morning of Sunday 3 October 1896, and was buried in the churchyard of Kelmscott in Oxfordshire on 6 October.

The obituaries and tributes were numerous and laudatory. Ironically, Morris's fight against the age had led to widespread recognition of at least some of the many facets of his achievement. *The Saturday Review*, long his adversary, now commissioned articles from Bernard Shaw, Arthur Symons (a leading literary critic) and R. B. Cunninghame Graham (a flamboyant radical writer and traveller). The last-mentioned wrote of the funeral, under the heading 'With the North-West Wind' – the rain and gale seeming in keeping with Morris's Viking personality. The account ends with the writer sharing for a moment Morris's vision :

John Ball stood by the grave, with him a band of archers all in Lincoln Green, birds twittered in the trees, and in the air the scent of apple-blossom and white hawthorn hung. All was fairer than I had ever seen the country look, fair with a fairness that was never seen in England but by the poet, and yet a fairness with which he laboured to endue it. Once more the mist descended, and my sight grew dimmer; the England of the Fellowship was gone. John Ball now vanished, and with him the order, and in their place remained the knot of countrymen, plough-galled and bent with toil; the little church turned greyer, as if a reformation had passed over it. I looked again, the bluff bold kindly face had faded into the north-west wind.

Perhaps, though, Morris – who had said of Cunninghame Graham that 'he's too bloody politeful' – would have preferred the less poetic tribute of the socialist journalist Robert Blatchford, who wrote in the *Clarion* :

I cannot help thinking that it does not matter what goes into the *Clarion* this week, because William Morris is dead . . . He was our best man, and he is dead.

Fortunately Morris's vision survives in his works, holding out to us from an age whose materialism and ruthlessness he so strenuously resisted the fruitful suggestion of

> To what a heaven the earth might grow
> If fear beneath the earth were laid
> If hope failed not, nor love decayed.

To have expressed that aspiration in 'The Love of Alcestis' was fine; to have lived so largely in its spirit was finer.

Epilogue

The influence of any writer or artist on his successors is always difficult to trace, and with someone so various as Morris the situation is particularly complicated. Moreover he would have been the last person to wish to separate his own influence from that of thinkers and designers whom he respected. Nevertheless, Morris has clearly been influential, and in two main areas: as an exponent of crafts, and as a social thinker.

On the first score, it is evident that the Arts and Crafts movement of the late nineteenth and early twentieth centuries evoked its initial inspiration from Morris's example. The belief that art should be applied to improving the quality of everything in ordinary life, rather than seeking a superior world of its own, led to a burgeoning of craft activity and organisation: in 1882 Arthur Mackmurdo founded the Century Guild; this was followed in 1884 by the Art Workers' Guild, and the Home Arts and Industries Association, stressing rural crafts; and in 1888 by C. R. Ashbee's Guild and School of Handicrafts, and the Arts and Crafts Exhibition Society. The quality of craftsmanship and design achieved by these groups and those associated with them like Walter Crane, W. R. Lethaby and C. F. A. Voysey was far higher than had been achieved in the mid-century because they shared Morris's sense of the need to respect the media in which they were working. The associated architectural development in Webb, Norman Shaw, Voysey and early works by Edwin Lutyens produced a number of distinguished country houses of great humanity, while Ebenezer Howard propounded and Raymond Unwin realised the idea of the Garden City. Edward Johnston revived the art of calligraphy, and Eric Gill became a great letterer and carver, as well as a social critic in the Morris tradition.

None the less, the products of the Arts and Crafts movement were expensive and consequently limited in their possible appeal. This was partly because of the emphasis on quality but mainly, as Nikolaus Pevsner argued in *Pioneers of Modern Design,* because of the movement's hostility to the machine. It needed, Pevsner shows, respect for craftsmanship to become allied with the engineering skills released by modern steel technology in order that the modern movement in design associated with the Bauhaus should come into being. In Pevsner's words, 'Morris laid the foundation of the modern style; with Gropius its character was ultimately determined'.[1] But since those words were written there has developed a good deal of scepticism about the activities of the modern movement in architecture, at least as it has manifested itself in postwar Britain. Many people feel that its uncompromising forms, especially in blocks of flats and offices, are inappropriate to human needs : that the style can too easily please the planners rather than those who have to live with it. With our increased awareness of the need for improvement of the environment and respect for nature, and above all of the fact that architecture must take its scale from man himself, there is a tendency to return to the ideals expressed by men like Morris, Lethaby and Ashbee. Indeed, Patrick Nuttgens has recently suggested that the ideas of the Arts and Crafts movement 'could inspire the next wave of social thinking and design'.[2] It is not so much Morris's specific designs that are significant here – though the success of Sandersons' reproduction of some of his wallpapers and fabrics in recent years shows that these still have a strong appeal – as his basic principles of respect for the material and awareness of the human function of whatever is made.

The second area in which Morris's influence has been felt – particularly since the 1930s – has been that of social and political thought. Bernard Shaw, G. D. H. Cole, Middleton Murry, Granville Hicks belong to this grouping, as do two of the most interesting postwar British socialist writers, Raymond Williams and Edward Thompson. Both Williams and Thompson have written well about Morris (the former in *Culture and Society* and the latter in his massive biography *William Morris. Romantic to Revolutionary*), but more significantly they – and especially Thompson – have seen in Morris's political thinking the potentiality for a humanising and enrichment of contemporary socialism. Mr Thompson's 'Postscript : 1976' in the new edition of his book argues that Marxists cannot simply claim Morris for their tradition : 'Morris may be assimilated to Marxism only in the course of self-criticism and re-ordering within Marxism itself.'[3] This is because Morris's work challenges the elevation of scientific over utopian socialism, and reminds us of the need to educate our desires by the use of our social imagination.

Morris would probably have been pleased to know that his influence had been strongest in these two areas, but he would have argued strongly that they are in fact one. His belief in craftsmanship, like his belief in socialism, is based on the view that it alone can fulfil fundamental human needs. He did not believe that men could be happy working in factories organised for mass production, and he believed that capitalism inevitably led to such a system. As he wrote, 'Nature will not finally be conquered until our work becomes part of the pleasure of our lives.' Perhaps mankind will never achieve this conquest; perhaps shorter hours of work and more time for gardening and Do-It-Yourself is all that most people can expect. But with the dwindling of the world's natural resources and an increasing sense that 'small is beautiful' we may soon be abandoning the assumption that industrial growth is the highest good. Morris, with his hatred of imperialism, would have been gratified that one of the clearest expositions of a social and political philosophy recognising these facts should have come from the Senegalese thinker Leopold Senghor. In *On African Socialism* Senghor has insisted that man must become 'not only a consumer, but above all a producer of culture'.[4] It is the development of that creative capacity that Morris convincingly argued to be mankind's deepest need. Here we can see the unity between these aspects of Morris's achievement and his creative writings. The early *Defence of Guenevere* poems give energetic expression to a sense of crisis, while those of *The Earthly Paradise* period suggest, despite their melancholy tone, the persistence of the human desire for happiness. In *Sigurd the Volsung* this is shown as something to be boldly fought for, and the value of courage is finely conveyed. In the prose romances Morris's idealism expresses itself fully in the adventures of his attractive characters, whose success in life is associated with their combination of humanity and a sense of their place in nature. Indeed, it is Morris's most profound insight, and one which underlies the whole spectrum of his astonishing creativity, that man is most completely human when he is able to see himself in the perspective of the natural universe.

Notes

PREFACE

1   W. B. Yeats, 'The happiest of the poets' (1903), in *Essays* (London, 1924), p. 77.
2   Edward Carpenter, in *Freedom*, X, December 1896, p. 118. This article is included in *William Morris. The Critical Heritage* edited by Peter Faulkner (London, 1973), pp. 401–3. Where no specific references are given subsequently, the sources are included in that volume.

CHAPTER 1

1   The complete letter is printed in Henderson, *Letters*, and Briggs, *Selected Writings*.
2   A. W. N. Pugin, *Contrasts; or a Parallel Between the Noble Edifices of the Middle Ages and the Corresponding Buildings of the Present Day* (London, 1836).
    For an account of the whole tradition see Alice Chandler, *A Dream of Order* (London, 1971); also Margaret Grennan, *William Morris Medievalist and Revolutionary*, (New York, 1945).
3   John Ruskin, *Stones of Venice*, Vol II, in *The Works of John Ruskin*, ed. E. T. Cook and A. Wedderburn, 39 vols (London 1903–12), Vol. X, p. 193.
4   *Collected Works*, Vol. XXII, p. xvii.
5   Mackail, Vol. I, pp. 45 and 63.
6   *Collected Works*, Vol. XXIII, p. 85.
7   *Memorials*, Vol. I, pp. 114–15.
8   They appear in *Collected Works*, Vol. I, and in the Everyman University Library edition, *Early Romances in Prose and Verse* by William Morris, ed. Peter Faulkner; the volume also includes *The Defence of Guenevere and other poems* (1858).
9   There is no full modern study of Webb, but W. R. Lethaby's *Philip Webb*, originally produced in 1935, is being reissued by the Acanthus Press in 1980.
10 A clear account of this matter is given by K. W. Goodwin, 'William Morris's "new and lighter design"', *Journal*, vol. II, no. 3, Winter 1968, pp. 24–31.
11 *The Ecclesiastic and Theologian*, Vol. XX, no. 62, March 1858, pp. 159–70. I am indebted to Dr Tom Drescher for this reference.
12 Andrew Lang, 'The poetry of William Morris', *Contemporary Review*, XLII, August 1882, pp. 200–17, esp. p. 202.
13 G. Saintsbury, *Corrected Impressions* (London, 1895), p. 213.
14 Apart from Pater's striking review, the best critical account of the volume remains Dixon Scott, 'The first Morris', in *Primitiae. Essays in English Literature*, by students of the University of Liverpool (London, 1912).

CHAPTER 2

1 See 'William Morris lived here', *Homes and Gardens*, vol. 59, no. 8, February 1978, pp. 34–9, and, for the relation of the house to other domestic designs, R. Dixon and S. Muthesius, *Victorian Architecture* (London, 1978), pp. 50–1.

2 *Memorials*, Vol. I, p. 212.

3 See Charlotte Gere's remark in the Catalogue to the exhibition of 'Morris & Company' at the Fine Art Society, April–May 1979, that 'Interest in his work and that of the remarkable artistic talents who collaborated with him in designing for Morris and Co., has probably never been so great as in the last ten years'.

No full history of the Firm (which lasted until 1940) has yet been written to supersede H. C. Marillier, *A Brief Sketch of the Morris Movement and of the Firm* . . . (London, 1911). But there are useful discussions of Morris and the Firm in the major books on this aspect of Morris: G. H. Crow, *William Morris, Designer* (London, 1934), and Raymond Watkinson, *William Morris as a Designer* (London, 1968).

4 I am deeply indebted for all my discussions of Morris's stained glass to A. C. Sewter's superb volumes, *The Stained Glass of William Morris and his Circle*, 2 vols (New Haven and London, 1974–5).

5 ibid., Vol. I, p. 88.

6 See Sydney Cockerell, 'Notes on Warington Taylor and Philip Webb', *Journal*, vol. I, no 2, Winter 1962, pp. 6–10.

7 See J. Y. Le Bourgeois, 'William Morris at St James's Palace : a sequel', *Journal*, vol. III, no. 1, Spring 1974, pp. 7–9.

8 W. M. Rossetti (ed.), *Rossetti Papers* (London, 1903), p. 505 (19 April 1870).

9 Mrs Russell Barrington, *Life of Walter Bagehot* (London, 1915, 1918), p. 412.

10 E. V. Lucas, *The Colvins and their Friends* (London, 1928), pp. 35–6.

11 H. Allingham and D. Radford (eds), *William Allingham. A Diary* (London, 1967), p. 316 (13 June 1882).

12 Mrs C. W. Earle, *Pot-Pourri from a Surrey Garden* (London, 1897, 1900), pp. 277–8.

13 M. Magnusson and H. Palsson, translators, *Laxdaela Saga* (Harmondsworth, 1969).

14 See D. M. Hoare, *The Work of Morris and Yeats in Relation to Early Saga Literature* (Cambridge, 1937), and R. C. Ellison, ' "The Undying Glory of Dreams" ', in *Victorian Poetry,* ed. M. Bradbury and D. Palmer (London, 1972), pp. 143–74.

15 Margaret Howitt (ed.), *Mary Howitt. An Autobiography*, 2 vols (London, 1889), Vol. II, p. 170 (17 March 1869).

16 *The Athenaeum*, no. 2251, 17 December 1870, pp. 795–7.

17 *The Christian Observer*, LXIX, March 1870, pp. 198–208, esp. pp. 207–8.

18 Elizabeth J. Hasell, *Blackwood's Magazine*, CVI, July 1869, pp. 56–73, esp. p. 73.

CHAPTER 3

1 See John Bryson (ed.), *Dante Gabriel Rossetti and Jane Morris: their Correspondence* (Oxford, 1976).

2 See J. Kocmanova, ' "Landscape and Sentiment"; Morris's first attempt in longer prose fiction', *Victorian Poetry*, vol. XIII, nos 3-4, Fall–Winter 1975, pp. 103-17.

3 See J. R. Dunlop, 'Morris and the book arts before the Kelmscott Press', ibid., pp. 141-57.

4 The journals have been published by James Morris: *Icelandic Journals by William Morris* (Fontwell, 1969).

5 Quoted by Peter Floud in 'The wallpaper designs of William Morris', in *The Penrose Annual* (London, 1960), p. 43.

6 W. R. Lethaby, *Philip Webb* (London, 1935), p. 94.

7 Henry Morley, 'Recent literature', *Nineteenth Century*, II, November 1877, pp. 704-12, esp. pp: 711-12.

CHAPTER 4

1 'William Morris, MA', *The Dublin University Magazine*, n.s. II, November 1878, pp. 552-68.

2 The manifesto is published in the *Letters*, Appendix II, and is quoted in Mackail, Vol. I, pp. 349-50.

3 Quoted in ibid., Vol. I, pp. 340-1.

4 Peter Floud was the first person to draw attention to this influence in 'Dating Morris patterns', *The Architectural Review*, July 1959, pp. 15-20.

5 Mackail, Vol. II, p. 37.

6 ibid., Vol. II, p. 57.

7 See Sewter, *Stained Glass*, Vol. I, p. 56.

8 The lectures constitute *Collected Works*, Vols XXII and XXIII; selections from them also appear in the volumes edited by Cole, Briggs and Morton.

9 See Orwell, 'Politics and the English language', in *Collected Essays, Journalism and Letters of George Orwell* ed. Sonia Orwell and Ian Angus (1968; Harmondsworth, 1970), Vol. IV, pp. 156-69.

10 Walter Hamilton, *The Aesthetic Movement in England* (London, 1882).

11 Andrew Lang, 'The poetry of William Morris', *Contemporary Review*, XLII, August 1882, pp. 200-17, esp. pp. 201-2.

12 Quoted by Mackail, Vol. II, pp. 15-16.

13 ibid., Vol. II, p. 21.

CHAPTER 5

1 E. P. Thompson, *William Morris* (London, 1977), p. 268.

2 See C. Tsuzuki, *H. M. Hyndman and British Socialism* (London, 1961).

3 For a subtle reading of *John Ball*, see John Goode, 'William Morris and the dream of revolution', in *Literature and Politics in the Nineteenth Century*, ed. John Lucas (London, 1971).

4 'The poet in the police-court', *Saturday Review*, LX, September 1885, p. 417.

5 Quoted in Sewter, *Stained Glass*, Vol. II, p. 20.

6 Peter Floud, 'Dating Morris patterns', *Architectural Review*, July 1959, pp. 14–20.

7 'On the Wandle' in *Spectator*, LVI, November 1883, pp. 1507–9.

8 Emma Lazarus, 'A day in Surrey with William Morris', *Century Magazine*, XXXII, July 1886, pp. 388–97.

9 R. Y. Tyrrell, *Quarterly Review*, CLXIX, July 1889, pp. 111–13.

10 Edward Bellamy, *Looking Backward 2000–1887* (New York, 1888).

11 The best recent account of *News from Nowhere* is by John Goode; see note 3 above.

12 F. S. Marvin in *William Morris 1834–1934. Some Appreciations* (Walthamstow, 1934), p. 26.

13 Bruce Glasier, *William Morris*, p. 23.

14 Friedrich Engels to Paul and Laura Lafargue in Engels's *Correspondence*, 2 vols (Moscow, 1959).

15 Morris to Dr John Glasse, 23 September 1887; in R. Page Arnot, *William Morris, the Man and the Myth* (London, 1964), p. 83.

CHAPTER 6

1 Bruce Glasier, *William Morris*, pp. 116–17.

2 Ernest Rhys, *Everyman Remembers* (London, 1931), pp. 48–9.

3 Published in May Morris (ed.), *William Morris: Artist, Writer, Socialist* (Oxford, 1936), Vol. II, and by the William Morris Society (1966).

4 W. B. Yeats, *Autobiographies* (1955), pp. 139–49.

5 Elizabeth R. Pennell, *The Life and Letters of Joseph Pennell*, 2 vols (London, 1930), Vol. I, pp. 158–9.

6 Burne-Jones, *Memorials*, Vol. II, p. 278.

7 Sewter, *Stained Glass*, Vol. I, p. 57.

8 *The Studio* (September 1893).

9 'The question of the Laureateship', *The Bookman*, III, November 1892, pp. 52–5.

10 Mackail, Vol. II, p. 288.

11 Oscar Wilde, 'The decay of lying', in *The Works of Oscar Wilde*, ed. G. F. Maine (London, 1948, 1954), p. 913.

12 *The Wood Beyond the World*, Dover Publications (New York, 1972).

13 Gabriel Mourey, *Across the Channel. Life and Art in London*, trans. Georgina Latimer (London, 1896), pp. 147–56.

14 Burne-Jones, *Memorials*, Vol. II, p. 265.

15 ibid., Vol. II, p. 277.

EPILOGUE

1 Nikolaus Pevsner, *Pioneers of Modern Design* (1936; Harmondsworth, 1960), ch. 1, p. 39.

2 Patrick Nuttgens, 'A full life and an honest place', in *Spirit of the Age*, ed. John Drummond (London, 1976), p. 213.

3 E. P. Thompson, *William Morris* (London, 1977), p. 802.

4 Leopold Senghor, 'Nationhood' (1959), in *On African Socialism*, trans. and intr. Mercer Cook (New York, 1964), p. 51.

Suggested Reading

TEXTS

The Works of William Morris, ed. with prefaces by May Morris in 24 volumes (London: Longmans Green, 1910–15), will be found in the larger libraries. They are supplemented by two further volumes edited by May Morris entitled *William Morris: Artist, Writer, Socialist* (Oxford: Blackwell, 1936), and by E. D. LeMire, *The Unpublished Lectures of William Morris* (Detroit: Wayne State University Press, 1969).

Early Romances in Prose and Verse by William Morris, ed. Peter Faulkner (London: Dent, 1973).

News from Nowhere, ed. James Redmond (London: Routledge & Kegan Paul, 1970).

The Wood Beyond the World (fascimile of Kelmscott Press edn) (New York: Dover Publications, 1972).

Most of Morris's writings are available only in selections such as Asa Briggs (ed.), *William Morris. Selected Writings and Designs* (Harmondsworth: Penguin, 1962); G. D. H. Cole (ed.), *William Morris. Selected Writings* (London: Nonsuch Press, 1934, 1948); Geoffrey Grigson (ed.), *A Choice of William Morris's Verse* (London: Faber, 1969); A. L. Morton (ed.), *Three Works by William Morris* (London: Lawrence & Wishart, 1968); and *Political Writings of William Morris* (London: Lawrence & Wishart, 1973).

Letters

Philip Henderson (ed.), *Letters of William Morris to his Family and Friends* (London: Longmans Green, 1950); a full edition of Morris's letters is being prepared by Professor Norman Kelvin.

SECONDARY SOURCES

There are many books about Morris and various aspects of his achievements which may prove of interest to the student. Of the many I would particularly recommend the following.

Biography

J. W. Mackail, *The Life of William Morris*, 2 vols (London: 1899).

Philip Henderson, *William Morris, his Life, Work and Friends* (London: Thames & Hudson, 1967).

Jack Lindsay, *William Morris. His Life and Work* (London: Constable, 1975).

Political Biography
E. P. Thompson, *William Morris: Romantic to Revolutionary* (London: Lawrence & Wishart, 1955; Merlin Press, 1977).

Design
G. H. Crow, *William Morris, Designer* (London: Studio Books, 1934).
Raymond Watkinson, *William Morris as a Designer* (London: Studio Vista, 1968).

Stained Glass
A. C. Sewter, *The Stained Glass of William Morris and his Circle*, 2 vols (New Haven and London: Paul Mellon Centre, 1974–5).

Contemporary Reviews
Peter Faulkner (ed.), *William Morris. The Critical Heritage* (London: Routledge & Kegan Paul, 1973).

General Criticism
Paul Thompson, *The Work of William Morris* (London: Heinemann, 1967).
Morris number of *Victorian Poetry*, vol. XIII, nos 3–4, Fall–Winter 1975.

Journal
The Journal of the William Morris Society.

Exhibitions and Churches
Morris's work can be seen in the William Morris Gallery at Walthamstow, and the Victoria and Albert Museum, London, and in other museums and galleries. Students should watch out for notices of relevant exhibitions, and for stained glass by the Firm in churches in various parts of the country. (These will be indicated in reputable guide books like Nikolaus Pevsner's Buildings of England series; there is also a gazetteer in Paul Thompson's *The Work of William Morris*.)

Index

de Morgan, William 107, 125
Dickens, Charles 5, 84, 101, 175;
  Bleak House 98; *Our Mutual
  Friend* 98, 153
Disraeli, Benjamin 87, 90, 91, 111;
  Sibyl 111
Dixon, R. W. 5, 6, 8
dreams 10, 12, 100–1, 105, 120, 132,
  133, 143
Dresser, Christopher 35, 36; *Prin-
  ciples* 73
Dublin University Magazine 89
dyeing 63, 66, 74, 93, 125

Earl, Mrs C. W., *Pot Pourri from a
  Surrey Garden* 37
Early English Text Society 50
Eastern Question Association 85, 87,
  88, 89, 90, 91
Ecclesiastic and Theologian 24
Edinburgh Review 156
Eliot, George 35, 101, 165, 175
Eliot, T. S. 46
Ellis, F. S. 44, 158
embroidery 29, 30, 74, 107
Engels, Friedrich 5, 112, 113, 144
English Illustrated Magazine 132
Epping Forest 1, 3
Evangelicalism 1, 4
Evans, W. H. 67
Exeter College 2, 5

Fabian Society 113, 128–9, 153
Faulkner, Charles 30, 33, 66, 71, 75,
  81, 144
Figaro 175
Floud, Peter 123
Ford, Ford Madox, *Ancient Lights*
  149
Forman, H. Buxton 58
Fortnightly Review 25, 51, 66, 101,
  105
Fraser's Magazine 23
Freedom x
Froissart, Jean 16, 17, 20, 24, 38, 44
furniture 30, 35, 89

Garnett, Richard 24
Gaskell, Elizabeth 5
Gaskin, Arthur 157
Gere, C. M. 157
Germ, The 9
Gill, Eric 179

Gissing, George 165, 167
Gladstone, William Ewart 111, 164
Glasier, John Bruce 133; *Early Days
  ...* 117, 144, 146, 147, 149
Glasse, Dr John 145
Goethe, J. W. von 22
Gothic 6, 8, 9, 11, 27, 28, 96, 104,
  107
Gothic Revival 65
Green Dining Room 34–5
Grettis Saga 51
Grimm, Johann, *Der Eisenhaus* 65
Guy, Rev. F. B. 4

Hamilton, Walter, *The Aesthetic
  Movement in England* 107
Hammersmith Socialist Society 146,
  147–8
Hardy, Keir 147
Hardy, Thomas 164; *Jude the
  Obscure* 119
Hasell, Elizabeth 58
Hewlett, Maurice 133, 138
Hicks, Granville 180
High Church 2, 4, 7, 30
Hollamby, Edward 28
Hopkins, Gerard Manley 50, 164
Horace, *Odes* 66
Horner 153; *The Odyssey* 129
Howard, Ebenezer 179
Howitt, Mary 55
Hunt, William Holman 9, 60
Huxley, Thomas Henry 153
Hyndman, H. M. 111, 113, 117, 118,
  152–3; *Record of an Adventurous
  Life* 25

Iceland 50, 66, 67, 75
Icelandic heroes 70, 174
Icelandic literature 50, 51, 62, 67,
  84, 118, 164
illuminated manuscripts 8, 65

Jacobins 112
James, Alice 59
James, Henry 45, 59–61, 175
Jeffrey and Co. 31
Jingoism 90
Johnson, Florence 74
Johnson, Lionel 133, 138
Johnston, Edward 179
Jones, Owen 35, 36, 73; *Grammar of
  Ornament* 30

INDEX